I Will Sing Life

I will

Sing Life

Voices from the
Hole in the Wall Gang Camp

With an Introduction by
Paul Newman

By Larry Berger, Dahlia Lithwick, and
Seven Campers

Photographs by Robert Benson

Little, Brown and Company
Boston   Toronto   London

After expenses, the authors' and photographer's earnings from the book, as well as a portion of the publisher's profits, will be directed to The Teddy Bear Fund, Inc., which was established for the benefit of the Hole in the Wall Gang Camp. For more information about the camp, please contact:

The Hole in the Wall Gang Fund, Inc.
555 Long Wharf Drive
New Haven, CT 06511
(203) 772-0522

First Edition

Library of Congress Cataloging-in-Publication Data

I will sing life : voices from the Hole in the Wall Gang Camp / by Larry Berger, Dahlia Lithwick, and seven campers : photographs by Robert Benson : with an introduction by Paul Newman. — 1st ed.

    p.   cm.

    Summary: Seven children with life-threatening illnesses share their perspectives on life.

    ISBN 0-316-09273-8

    1. Children's writings, American—Connecticut.   2. Sick children—Literary collections. [1. Sick—Literary collections. 2. Children's writings.] I. Berger, Larry. II. Lithwick, Dahlia.   III. Benson, Robert, ill.
    PS548.C8I17   1992
    818'.540809282—dc20   91-46203

10 9 8 7 6 5 4 3 2 1

RRD-IN ·

Design by Barbara Werden

Published simultaneously in Canada by Little, Brown & Company (Canada) Limited

Printed in the United States of America

Contents

~~~~~~

I wish there was a bird from God
and got me well
from His wings on me,
and got me well.

JASON ORCUTT, age nine

Introduction

∿∿∿∿∿∿∿∿∿∿

MAKE NO MISTAKE about it. This book does not fall into the category of grief and anguish. Both are most certainly present in large doses, but for me at least, the force of the book, the pages that carry lasting wallop, have to do with the strengthening of hope, the compression of wisdom, and, if you'll bear with me, the violation of a well-known natural law, which states: "You only gits back what you puts in."

There are several elements that came together to forge this book. Let me start with the Hole in the Wall Gang Camp, not because it was the most important, but because it was there first. The name comes from that legendary hideout for Butch Cassidy and the Sundance Kid. The campers are children from seven to seventeen years of age who have or have had life-threatening diseases.

I wish I could recall with clarity the impulse that compelled me to help bring this camp into being. I'd be pleased if I could announce a motive of lofty purpose. I've been accused of compassion, of altruism, of devotion to Christian, Hebrew, and Moslem ethic, but however desperate I am to claim ownership of a high ideal, I cannot.

I wanted, I think, to acknowledge Luck: the chance of it, the benevolence of it in my life, and the brutality of it in the lives of others; made especially savage for children because they may not be allowed the good fortune of a lifetime to correct it.

But whatever the impetus, the place exists. It wasn't so much built — it simply exploded into operation out of other people's generosity. It magically collected everything: canoes, a swimming pool, volunteers, architects, doctors, fishing tackle, nurses, a pig, snakes, an amphitheater, food, loyalty — an endless list.

I Will Sing Life

And letters — this one, sent home by a counselor, found its way from there to me:

It's hard to explain how a camp for children with serious illnesses can be the happiest place I've ever been, but everyone here agrees that it's true. The counselors at the camp are mostly college students: English, economics, music majors, from all around the country. Most have had no experience with special populations at all. Every session volunteers join us from all around the world — advertising executives, plumbers, and priests — all giving two weeks of their vacation time to the campers. Most of the counselors come armed with a love of kids, a love of camp, a natural terror of disease, and a couple of books about coping with grief bought in a panic the previous week. Those books usually gather dust in the bottom of their duffel bags.

It is true that the night before the campers first arrived, most of the staff walked around hollow-eyed, perhaps reading a Bible or canoeing out to the middle of the lake to wonder why there is such a thing as sickness, asking each other frightening "what if . . ." questions. We braced ourselves for the tears and the fears of the sad, sick children about to arrive.

But as the first activity began, the poor darlings, who had been handled delicately all afternoon by their terrified counselors, each got a balloon attached to an ankle and were gathered together on the tennis courts. Their mission: to jump, leap, poke, and pop everyone else's balloon while preserving their own. Kids with crutches fly around jabbing at everything and everyone they see; kids in wheelchairs pop wheelies timed to the right second and perfect angle that will allow a front wheel to snag a balloon, or a foot. The hemophiliacs, who should be avoiding bruises, roll around on the ground, clobbering one another. The counselors lose track, forget names, start to laugh, and begin to relax. What moments ago seemed fragile and foreign is the lone triumphant teenager with the immense grin who has managed to keep the orange balloon at his feet intact. . . .

This may give the impression that everyone thinks the kids are the only beneficiaries. But then I remember the first year when we were shaky and every hour critical. A counselor moaned: "I'm wrecked. The day is tough enough, but Lordie, the middle of the night, they're scared or hurt and they pile into my bed. I'm getting no sleep. None!"

Then the end of the season.

ME: How's it goin'?
HIM: Good.
ME: Sleeping any?
HIM: It's nuts. I can't get to sleep until I get them all stacked on top of me.

Two years ago, two young students, Dahlia Lithwick and Larry Berger, fresh from their junior year at Yale, came to the camp. They came armed with a poetry program, the secret of which, in their words, was as follows:

We never suggested that the campers write about being sick. We simply encouraged them to stretch their imaginations, play around, make up words, use slang, and never worry about spelling. We would sit in the woods by the lake and write odes to camp food, haiku about fungi, rap songs about counselors. We wanted the poetry program to be, like the rest of camp, a place where sick kids could laugh at the same things that make normal kids laugh.

But once the campers realized that the poetry program was as safe and fun as the rest of camp, they started using it as a forum for expressing deeper things that they had never been able to say to their moms, their psychologists, or their doctors. They could do this because the camp is much more than a place where sick kids get to be normal. It is also the one place in their lives where it is normal to be sick. At camp they are *supposed* to have a disease, so they know that no one will pity, analyze, or be afraid of what they write or say about it. At camp they can stop explaining their illnesses, and start exploring the rest of their lives.

Writing poetry is ideal for this exploration because it offers the campers a world in which, rather than being controlled by the "can'ts" and "don'ts" of illness, they control the "what ifs?" of imagination. Camp is an ideal place for this kind of poetry, because if things ever get too intense, they can always take a break and go fishing.

The poetry stunned everyone and there followed a recommendation that the poems be collected into a book. Dahlia and Larry decided that the best way to do this was to put the poems in the context of the children's lives. They spent a month in each child's home, and hospital, living with the family, building the trust they already had established at camp, meeting friends, doctors, and siblings.

On the following pages, a compendium of vivid dialogue, you will be in the company of seven young campers. You will acquaint yourself with their imagination and their poetry; be made aware of their virtues and flaws, their fears, doubts, and vanities, the diversity of their interests and aspirations. But finally I think you will be struck by the intensity of the life that they experience, amazed at the toughness of their perception, and humbled by their forgiveness.

With all that said, I'd be delinquent if I didn't give you a taste. This one was chosen not because it was the most important or best, but because it was the first poem Dahlia and Larry handed me.

*If I am alone
There is a clear and empty
Blank sky.
If I am with you I see blinking, shining, beautiful
Stars in my heart.*

*When I am alone
In the forest
I see only woods
But when I'm with you I see nature.*

Last night you looked like a dancing violet in the wind.

The poet, at the time, was seven.

My wife, Joanne, told me of another poet, as yet unpublished. His name was Germaine, and I remember him as being about ten. He came to us neither strong nor mobile, so he was taken from activity to activity in a golf cart. Later, with the help of a counselor, he was allowed to drive himself. He made a point of picking up the ladies. As his driving improved and his reputation as Lothario grew, why so did he.

One breezy day he saw my wife in the distance, accelerated briskly, came alongside, and smiled his Great Lothario Smile. Joanne smiled back, and the poet, under full sail, said, "Yo, babe! Get in the car!" There is surprise and confidence here.

Paul Newman

WITH THE EXCEPTION of our chapter introductions, everything that follows is in the children's own words. We condensed the chapters from conversations recorded during the month we spent with each child at home and during the summers we spent with them at camp. The children worked with us on organizing and revising their chapters.

While we sometimes used listening to music, nature walks, and imagination games to help them find subjects for their poems and stories, we limited our participation in their writing process to suggesting lines that might need revision. When they got stuck, we would ask them questions, play more games, and discuss other poems that could get them inspired again. Adam, Shawn, Pia, and Katie often preferred to compose their poems and stories orally, in which case we did the transcribing for them.

We join the children in dedicating this book to their extraordinary families.

Dahlia Lithwick and Larry Berger
Paupacken Lake, Pennsylvania

Adam Jed

ON THE TRAIL to his favorite clearing in the woods at camp, Adam is arguing that there is insufficient evidence for believing in God. He is, as usual, so excited about what he is saying that he does not inhale until the last possible instant. Then he dashes back into the sentence, accelerating to make up for the lost time.

When we reach the clearing, he parks his wheelchair and changes the subject. "Larry, what's it like being a camp counselor?"

"We work hard here, but it seems that no matter how much we put into this camp, we take out even more."

"But isn't that impossible? I mean, if everybody takes out more than they put in — " He stops and scratches his chin. "Well, maybe God is what puts in the extra."

Adam's genius always seeks "the extra" that could replace what was taken from him. It is the extra energy that would have run around his amputated legs and fingers that rushes instead to illuminate his thoughts, his eyes, and his laughter.

Adam is eight years old, and there are oaks, poplars, and maples in this clearing; but he will not climb them. He has come to write poems.

There are also raspberries, spiders, lichens, and sky in this clearing; but Adam will not write about them. He has come to write about trees, as he does in all of his nature poems. There is a deep kinship between Adam and his trees. The beauty of trees is undiminished by their loss of fingers in the fall, or limbs in storms. Trees cannot move like the other creatures, but that is why they are able to hold so much life and song. The trees in Adam's poems hold the burden of his memories, while his eight-year-old imagination climbs into their highest branches.

I Will Sing Life

THESE moments with his trees are among the few in which the lawyer in Adam lets the poet in Adam get a word in edgewise. Four years of preparation for his personal injury suit have honed Adam's astonishing legal mind. He already knows what kind of furniture he wants to have in the Adam Jed, Esq. corporate offices. As Adam finishes his poem and prepares to write its title, his attention jumps to a pressing legal matter, "Is it against the law for the same author to write two different poems with the same title?"

Sometimes, the lawyer and the poet in Adam challenge each other. In the opening poem of his chapter, Adam Jed, Esquire, puts poetry itself on trial for its crimes.

Just when the counselors at camp have decided that it is impossible that Adam is only eight years old, Dahlia happens to see him in the dining hall with tears in his eyes. She asks him if he wants to talk, but he just blows his nose and says, "I miss my mom."

~~~~~~

The Poetry Trial

Name?

   Imagination.

Occupation?

   Thinking.

Where do you live?

   In people's minds, outdoors, on pages of books, in shady pine trees, dead trees that are hunched over, and when people first wake up in the morning.

Where were you last night?

   In someone's dreams — a guy in a Jaguar wanted to rearrange some factory worker's neurosystems.

Do you have a criminal background?

   I sort of trespass on people's lives. I've made some people commit suicide, made some people go nuts, I speed through people's heads and park illegally in people's minds, double-park in front of the place where logic is parked, and I can rob your head and then give to the uncreative.

What weapons do you have?

   Small bush grenades, bullet rocks, sky nets, bees like a knife, trees like a lead pipe, poison lava, I throw nouns that conquer literature, I lead gangs of mean, wild adjectives, and attacking verbs, pronouns disguise themselves — he, she, they leave no trace — Mafia links of rhymes which could involve crimes.

Are you for real?

DEFENSE LAWYER: Your honor, I object. The prosecuting attorney is
   asking a non-expert for an opinion.
JUDGE: Sustained.

Do you have a family?

   Poetry is my grandparent, literature is my father, stories are
my brothers and sisters, my children are trees, bushes, and
dreams, my aunts and uncles are thoughts about what you think,
my cousin is Pascal who made a fortune gambling and invented
the grid. The two people who know his system aren't even allowed in casinos.

Do you have a good job?

   I'm a fictional writer, an environmental lawyer prosecuting a
toxic-waste dumper, a neurosurgeon with patients who can't
think imaginatively, who have TV-itis, and a garbage man who
throws out logic, a very lousy chess player only good at invent-
ing an opening, an English teacher, an artist who makes
futuristic paintings of shapes and squiggles.

Have you ever been to the First National Bank?

   In people's minds who have wishes to go into a money vault
and swim in the money.

Did you commit this bank robbery?

   No.

Can you stare into my eyes and say you did not do it?

   Yes.

CLOSING STATEMENT: I think he didn't do it, but even if he did, he's
probably just going to lie.

MY parents were in a lawsuit, because of my illness, but I'm not supposed
to discuss it. I know about it because I kind of peeked into a confidential
file that was kind of labeled "lawsuit." My parents' lawyers were the first
real lawyers I ever met. They gave me a T-shirt that says, "Adam Jed Future
Esquire," and then on the back it says, "My lawyer could beat up your lawyer." One thing I can say, though, is that I'd trade all the money in the
world to have my legs and fingers back.

   I want to be the richest, most famous lawyer in the world when I
grow up. I read *U.S. News* to find out about colleges and I've decided to
go to Yale undergraduate and then to Harvard for a combined business

and law degree. But they better get a little more wheelchair accessible before I come there. I took a kids' law class at a local college last summer and it was the most unaccessible place. There was a level below the ground, a level above the ground, but no level *on* the ground. Maybe they built it that way so that if there's a flood you're either saved or you drown; nobody gets wet and suffers.

I got four out of five questions right on Dahlia's practice Law School Admissions Test, which is better than she did and she just graduated from college. But she might get into law school anyway because I wrote her a nice recommendation. I love practical jokes, so when I saw her law school application forms I told her that I would be happy to give her a recommendation if she needed one. Then I went into the other room and wrote this:

> Dahlia Lithwick is an average IQed person. I wouldn't exactly
> call her even close to brillyent. She brings up obnoxshush sub-
> jects and things a lot. When I spent two weeks with her she
> minorly blackmailed me. Dahlia blabs a lot of gosip. Dahlia

thinks in a crazy way. I think Dahlia would be best to go to law school in a mental institution.

Adam Jed, *her lawyer*

I used lousy spelling because Dahlia is a really good speller and I didn't want them to think that she had written it. But then I decided that she probably wouldn't be that bad a lawyer so I steamed open the envelope and put in a nice recommendation instead.

WHEN I was at camp two years after I got sick, I wrote this poem. I didn't realize when I wrote it that you could match it up with what happened to me when I got sick. It was the first poem I ever wrote. My counselor was pushing my chair on the trail to where we write poetry and when he tipped me back to get over a stump, he lost his grip for a second and my heart sped up:

When the Tree Falls Down

When the tree falls down
On the ground and
Its heart speeds up
All that's left is
Memories and a very
Pretty cup.

In the cup are
Memories of storms
Times it was almost cut
Down and when it was
Young having fun with
Its parents.

When its cup of
Memories breaks
And its faith cracks
All that's left of it
Are very beautiful
Naps of thoughts.

I remember waking up that morning, I was perfectly fine, but then when I was in kindergarten I had the chills and I wanted to put on my jacket. Later that afternoon I was really sick and I threw up a couple of times. My dad came to pick me up and he said he had never seen me look so sick. I was shivering so much I didn't want to take my jacket off and my legs and ankles ached. I asked my mom to take me to the doctor, which is something I never did before. The doctor examined me. When I got home, I lay down in my mom's bed and I fell asleep. I slept through dinner and then my parents tried to wake me up, but I was mumbling under my breath and saying things that didn't make sense and I was still feverish. My mother spoke to the doctor again. My temperature was 103°. Other times when I had been sick I had temperatures as high as 105° and I ran around the house, but this time my ankles were hurting so much I couldn't even stand up.

My parents gave me a sponge bath and then put me to bed. As they were putting my pajamas on, they noticed a purple spot on my knee, but

*I will
Sing Life*

they thought I must have just banged it at school. That night they checked on me every twenty minutes. At 2:00 in the morning they decided to give me another sponge bath. When they took off my pajamas, they saw purple spots all over me, so they called my doctor. He said, "Meet me in the emergency room in ten minutes!" We rushed to the emergency room and all of a sudden people started putting tubes in me. My mom asked what it was and they said it was a deathly blood infection. I kept turning more and more purple.

I remember some details, like when they were sticking tubes in me and — this is funny — I asked if I would have to spend the night in the hospital; I ended up having to spend most of the year in the hospital! I remember the exact pajamas I was wearing; they had little footballs on them and they were a kind of brownish red. I remember the siren going off in the ambulance, but these are just little details. A lot of the time I was conscious, but sometimes I kept my eyes closed and some of it I can't remember. This is the sad part. My dad had stayed at home to watch my little sister, but my mom called him and told him to come to the hospital because she wanted him to see me before I died.

The disease is called meningococcemia. It's a weird word. It's a bacteria that is carried by lots of people but they are immune to it. Some people carry it for years and then suddenly lose their immunity and get really sick. It's very rare and scientists don't know why it happens. If my parents hadn't gotten me to the hospital, I would have died by the next morning, because my body was in shock.

For a report I did in school, I read a study in *Scientific American Medicine* that said that there are nine symptoms which predict the chances of a meningococcemia patient surviving. If you have three of them, you have a poor chance of living. If you have four or five, you have almost 100 percent mortality. I had eight out of the nine symptoms.

The really deathly symptom that I got is something called DIC — disseminated intravascular coagulation. It's the reason I was turning purple. *Disseminated* means all over, *intravascular* means in your veins (but actually this was just in my capillaries), and *coagulation* means clot. So I was bleeding through my skin while my blood was clotting, which was a couple of problems. There was a medicine called Heprin that could stop the clotting but would make the bleeding worse. If they gave me too much, I could bleed to death; if they didn't give me enough, I could clot to death. They gave me as much as they could, but the clotting still kept the blood from getting to my fingers and legs.

A few hours later they transferred me to a pediatric ICU at another

hospital. I was transferred there by an ambulance; my parents got to ride behind with their flashers on. For the first few days I was half-conscious. I remember every once in a while I was so thirsty that I drank like thirteen cans of Coke in one hour. I just knew I was major sick. My parents were saying, "Keep fighting, you're doing good, keep on going." I was too dazed at first, then I was sleeping a lot, and then I just didn't really care what was going on. It wasn't until later that I could think about whether I might have died.

After two weeks, even though I wasn't burned, they transferred me to a burn unit because of all the incredible skin death and all the organ damage. I remember before the amputations I'd look at my legs and I couldn't really feel them. I could only barely move them, and they were all black and blue. I figured maybe I'd bruised myself really bad. Most of the time they were covered by bandages.

Then on November 18 they did the amputations. With all the clotting, there just wasn't enough blood supply in the limbs to keep them alive, and if they didn't amputate I could have died from an infection. My par-

I will Sing Life

ents tried to tell me what was going to happen the day before the amputations, but I was just too dazed from the medication.

I remember the first day after the amputations, when I saw my parents, I was really mad. I mean, I gave it to them. Back then I wasn't into the law, but I wanted to throw something at them that they would think of for a long time, so I said, "I think I could sue you that you didn't consult me! I'm suing you; you're in big trouble. You had no right to do this! I'm never going to speak to you again." I mean, at the time I was really thinking, "I'll never be able to do this again or that again. I'll never be able to walk again." Back then I didn't even know that there were such things as fake legs. I thought I'd have to live my life like that. I was so mad I wished they had just let me die. I think I was just missing my legs.

If the hospital had asked me to sign a consent, I would have immediately said, "No," but then my parents would have started giving me advice and I probably would have ended up going with what they said. It was a hard decision. Sometimes, usually when I'm sad or worried about the future, I still wish they hadn't signed it.

I remember my dad telling me that it was my mom's birthday two days after the amputations and I asked the nurse if she would tape a crayon to my arm so I could make her a card.

I had about nine operations in the burn unit, mainly skin grafts and knee flaps. A skin graft is when they take skin from a part of your body and they put it on a different part of your body. The flaps are more major. For my right knee flap they flipped skin and muscle and fat over from a different part of my knee to cover the bottom of it; for my left they flipped it from below my leg.

I HAD to stay in the burn unit for three months. The visiting hours there were horrendous! Just a few hours during the day. I can understand keeping visitors out when they had to change bandages, but the rest of the time I would just sit there. My hands and legs were too bandaged up to do anything. That's when my dad taught me to play chess. My parents also hooked up a speaker phone in my hospital room and one in their room at home. They left them on all day and all night so that whenever I wanted to talk to them I could. I remember how I really wanted to go home, just to lie in my own bed for a while. I was forgetting what my house looked like, so my dad made a videotape of the whole house. Then later the doctors finally let me go home long enough to lie in my own bed for a couple of minutes, but then I had to go back.

I didn't really believe that I'd be able to walk again. I mean, I did not believe anybody. I basically stopped trusting anyone who had an M.D. after his name or anyone who had a white suit. I hadn't walked for so many months that even if I had my legs back, they would have been floppy as spaghetti. Then they fitted me for prosthetic legs. When I saw them, I figured it would be just like attaching the legs and I would walk great, but when I put them on and tried to walk — oh God! So first I did weight-lifting, then I went on parallel bars with the prosthetics, just strengthening my legs and working on my balance. Then I used a walker, then two canes, then one cane, then nothing. There were many times when it was so hard I wanted to give up, but different therapists and my parents got me to keep trying.

My first steps were fun, but it still seemed very hard. I'd say it was about eight or nine months from the amputations to when I first started to walk. Then it was another two weeks before I could walk up and down stairs, then it was about a year before I learned to run. Now I don't even have to think about it. Now, I jump, I leap, I gallop. I've never tried the special swimming prosthetics because I don't know how to swim. I want to get water legs so I can just walk in the water.

I go to a fitness club twice a week where I use the rowing machine, the bikes, and do a little weight-lifting and arm-wrestling with the therapist there. I can't beat most of the other kids at school with my left arm in arm-wrestling because the front part of my arm is really my back (they took muscle and skin and fat from my back to cover a hole in my arm in a ten-hour surgery), but I can still beat my sister Allison, even when she's using two hands and a chin.

Here's a story I made up about my prosthetics:

A Leg with an Ego

One day I stay at home because I am feeling sick, but my prosthetic legs decide to go to school alone, without me. Wearing black leather shoes and tannish pants, they walk through my school, go to my desk, sit down, and try to hold a pen with their feet. It doesn't work, and the paper falls off the desk. My whole class walks in and they all stare at the prosthetics. My teacher, Ms. Chapman, walks in, doesn't believe it, and collapses on the ground.

All the kids gather around her like a football team huddling and then one of the kids runs down to tell our principal, Mrs. Robinson, and she gives us recess for the rest of the day.

During recess my prosthetics play kickball. The person who's in charge of recess, Mrs. Rosenberg, comes by the kickball field, looks at the person who is kicking, and realizes it's just a pair of legs. She starts to run away, but she's so dizzy that she hits her face right into a fence. She gets up to go get Mrs. Robinson, but she slams her face against the wall and gets knocked out.

The students are sent home for the day because the teachers all fainted and there was no one to watch the kids at recess. So the legs get on the bus and put down their bookbag, but one of the kids tells the bus driver that the prosthetics don't have a seat belt on. She walks back, looks at the legs, and faints. So now there's no one to drive the kids home and they have to go to Mrs. Robinson. She calls our parents, but when my mom hears that my legs are at school without me, she faints. My pros-

thetics walk home, go into the house, up the stairs, and sit down
on my bed. When I see them, I faint. So the legs drive me to the
hospital. One leg pushes the pedal, the other leg turns the
steering wheel. There's a whole hospital emergency room filled
with all the people who have fainted.

Later, the prosthetics come in to visit me. They see me
walking around on another pair of prosthetics. They think that
I'm impersonating them and they get confused and faint.

Usually I'm on top of my prosthetics when the two of us go to school.
I can walk anywhere on them and I played Frisbee today at lunch. But I
can't play kickball as well as the prosthetics in my story. Only imaginary
prosthetics do that. No one in reality has ever fainted because of my prosthetics. A lot of the kids in school don't even know. I still hate having to
wear them — they're a real pain, and I can't lead as fast a life as I'd like.
It's difficult to go on sleep-overs at friends' houses if they've never seen
me without my legs.

My prosthetics are made of plastic and titanium. You can't just go into a store and buy them like shoes. I have to get fitted for them and they cost thousands of dollars. Putting them on takes me about ten minutes. First I put special socks over my stumps to protect them and I put my stumps in the socket of the leg. Then I take the sleeve, pull it up so that the rubber is against my leg and it creates suction that keeps them on. I wear them all day, but I take them off at night.

If I was going to invent the perfect prosthetics, I would make it so that when you put your stump in, the prosthetic socket actually adjusts around your stump. Early in the morning, your stump is going to be swollen; as it gets later, it's going to get smaller, but then when it gets really late, it's going to get swollen again. So the socket would have to adjust to the size of your stump. You'd never have to get a new pair of prosthetics because as you grow, it grows. Wouldn't that be great? And when you want to run, it'll give you lots of springiness, and when you want to walk, it would have less springiness. It would also be able to go in water. And while we're at it, maybe they could have thrusters on the feet, so you could fly. That would be really good for football. Somebody tries to tackle you, and you leap right over them!

Sometimes my prosthetics give me bad sores and I have to come home from school and start using my wheelchair. The wheelchair I've got is called a "Quickie 2." It's got cool plastic guards on the front, and you can get it in black and fluorescent pink, but I have black and blue.

Wheelchair

A tank used rarely but well in the war of differences.
Alone, a hippo.
With me, a cheetah.
On carpet, a snapping turtle attacking my sister.
On tile, a killing king cobra.

A big heavy harp playing jazz and rock and roll.
Alone, a fatty veal.
With me, the lightest matzoh ball consommé.
The beams, crossbars, doors and plumbing of the Empire State
    Building.

A pain in the neck that helps,
But because it helps it's a pain.

I sleep-wheel at night sometimes. I always keep my wheelchair by my bed, and sometimes I'll hop into it in the middle of the night while I'm still asleep and wheel it somewhere in the house. Once my dad saw me and asked, "Where are you going?" and I said, "Hawaii." I went to the kitchen and just sat there and then I left. In the morning I never remember any of it. It's dangerous because I could be dreaming that I was swimming in the ocean and wheel right down the steps.

I have to use my wheelchair for a long time after I get a bone revision. The bones in my legs grow faster than the skin, so they would poke right through the end of my leg if I didn't have surgery to make them shorter. The problem with bone revisions is that cutting the bone stimulates bone growth. I've heard from doctors that bone revisions are a lot more painful than internal-organ surgery and that they are as painful as an amputation. I don't remember the amputations very well, but I know they were very painful. I remember the bone revisions I had two years ago. For a couple of nights afterward I was screaming all night. They couldn't give me enough morphine. It's so painful because they're cutting through the

I Will Sing Life

skin, the flesh, and the bone. They cut through every nerve in your leg. I had one surgery, but it was on my left leg and on my right leg, so it was double the pain.

EVEN though I don't have them anymore, I can still feel my legs. I still have the nerves. If I woke up one night and I didn't know and couldn't see and couldn't hear, I would try to stand up. I can feel my nerves in my leg that could make my ankle bend and I still have the nerves that can feel my amputated fingers wiggle. I have such a deep habit of twitching one of my toe nerves or my ankle nerve. If I don't twitch it, it feels like I'm not breathing in my leg; it's kind of like I am holding my breath in my leg.

I wish that I could still feel things and do things with my legs, even something that wouldn't sound so good to you like feeling a sharp pin on my toes. I wrote this poem about my wish to be able to feel three things I used to feel:

The Snow Leopard

I see a snow leopard
Standing with his paws in front.
He's in a dark cave with snow
hanging from the ceiling.
"I can grant you the wish of feeling
like a true, natural human.
But wait! I must know what feeling
you want to be able to have."

"I want to be able to feel grass on my feet
like my hand running through my hair.
Sand tickling my toes
like a sneeze warning in my nose
Water sloshing against my legs
like when I ran through sprinklers."

"Good, then go now." He turned and at
the other side of the cave, he entered into
a large cavern of Spring.

I think kids have more wishes than grown-ups because kids haven't experienced much and there's a lot more things they'd like to be able to

do. Since I got sick, I have a lot of wishes relating to that. Before I got sick, the idea of a lot of money was like, "I don't need it, I'm okay," and still, I don't need it, but now I want it a little more, since I've gone through so much I want some constellation prizes.

Wishes help because they give me things to hope for. I have some impossible wishes, too. Like I wish this never happened to me. That's not possible unless they invent a time machine. But wishing that I could have my legs and fingers again, that is possible — I mean, they've got organ transplants and they're working on limb transplants. It's very possible that within the next ten to forty years they're gonna come up with limb transplants.

For me, it's life goes on. Something really bad happens, it happens, I try to adjust to it. It sort of bothers me when I stop and feel bad for myself. I just think, "Let me just go along with my friends, and do what I would do before. So, I'll do some things slightly different, but life goes on."

I'm not a person who cries a lot and it's not as if I try to hold it in. When I have emotional attacks and stuff like that, it's never at a time when I would be having fun; it's usually at a time when I'm just sitting and thinking, like at night when I'm trying to fall asleep. If there was a kid teasing me, I just keep thinking about it over and over. Or it might be something I could have done better at if this hadn't happened to me.

I remember after field day in our school, oh God, I did really awful on field day. They had races from 20 yards up to 600 yards, jump-roping, three-legged walking, and potato-sack races. Other years I hadn't even bothered to enter. Usually I just stayed home that day, but finally I decided, "Hey, I might as well, I mean, I know I'm not going to win, but I know I'm not going to come in last." And I didn't come in last. But a couple of weeks later I was just thinking about it and there's this one kid, he's a complete bragger, I would like to crush him like a walnut. He was saying, "I won this and I won that" and a lot of things came to my mind about what it would have been like if I hadn't gotten sick.

Usually when I think of my future I think of myself as being a successful lawyer or something like that, but when I'm being pessimistic I think of myself as, I don't know, I've got a job as a lawyer and things are hard, I get up in the morning and there's nothing special, nothing really interesting. Those are the times I usually have emotional attacks.

Eyes and Tears

The willow tree is like a man with a million eyes
and he cries
not because he has too many eyes
but because if you have too many eyes
you have too many tears.

A lot of people who get sick really need someone to believe in and they believe in God. Even before I was sick I didn't think there is a God and I still don't. I think if you can't see Him and you can't hear Him, He's probably not there. And if He is there but He's got no control then He's just a feeling you get. Other people might need a feeling, but I think everything is just things that happen scientifically, people's brains' actions. The way I think God happened was that some person came along and started religion, he just felt it was something he needed. Maybe he had a friend whose name happened to be God, and he decided that everybody should have a really good friend like God. When the man whose name was God died, everyone still had someone left to believe in. God could have been a woman too, like Goddess, and he just shortened it.

THERE are a lot of things I've learned because this happened to me. Before I got sick, it might just have been because I was young, but I wanted to do things that were really risky. Like I thought I wanted to be a basketball player. After being sick, I learned more about real life. Instead of going out and playing football and stuff that is not going to help you when you're older — I doubt any of my friends are going to make it to the Giants — I do more things that will help me in the real world, like politics, current events, chess, things that help me think instead of strengthening muscles.

I don't think I would have a nickname of Encyclopedia Jed if that did not happen to me. In class, my teacher will bring up a subject and I'll just start talking and talking. I like to collect a lot of information and then spit it out all at once. My teacher mentions an I.V. and I bring up a whole thing about a hospital and ten procedures I've read about in magazines and everything I know about medicine. When we're in science, I bring up everything I've ever read in my life. We were talking about the budget deficit and the teacher said that the only thing we can do is raise taxes, so

obviously I had to say something — I mean, I couldn't just sit there. So I opened my mouth and said, "Yeah, but if you raise taxes people are going to have less money to buy things, the economy is going to be worse, and you can't raise taxes again because it'll keep on happening, and we'll go into a really bad recession."

I WROTE this poem about the difference between the things that seem important in math class and the imaginary world of a dream:

In Numeral Worlds

In numeral worlds,
Black and white,
Parts of numbers,
Black fractions, white decimals.

As I enter the dream, everything seems to change.
Fractions are tropical flowers,
And decimals are colorful parrots.
Pebbles are like red boulders.
Life is like last things in the real world.
The wise dodo birds talk about, "Why do
You speak in a colorful manner and in brilliant feeling?"

When I re-enter the real world once again I've learned:
Pay more attention to small things,
Let the larger things find you.

I make sure to get good grades in school, so I can get into a good college that will help me be a great lawyer. I am hoping I can take the issue of hush clauses to the Supreme Court after I get out of law school. Hush clauses keep people from talking about a trial or a settlement in a lawsuit. I think it's unconstitutional. You should have your freedom of speech.

I'm pretty sure I want to be a lawyer, but there are a lot of other things that I'm good at. I think a lot about going into business, and in second grade I started a corporation with my best friend, Ryan. I made myself Chairman of the Board and made him President just to stay safe, so that he wouldn't take it over. Of course, he ended up running the company and there was no way I could fire him. It went completely nuts and we argued and argued. Finally, our staff quit and we went bankrupt. We set it up again and we went bankrupt again. Political? The political stuff was so bad I even hired a few kids as bodyguards. They did it in exchange for free chess lessons, and I think they just liked the idea of a job. When people ask if we ever made any profit at all, I tell them yeah, we made a ten-figure profit: zero, zero, zero, zero . . .

I'm also considering a career as a singer. If I had a choice, I'd prefer to be a vocalist, like Kathie Lee, or Barry Manilow, instead of a rock singer. I tried to put a kid's band together to go on *Star Search* with Ed McMahon, but we had some disagreements and they quit. I'm looking for new kids now. And me and my cabin at camp did a really great performance of Elvis singing "Blue Suede Shoes" for the camp talent show this summer. We all did that weird dance he did. I started taking trombone lessons, too. I would have liked to play the cello or the violin, but I wouldn't be able to push down the strings and hold the bow at the same time.

I have two really best friends. Ryan, the guy I started the corporation with, and Jessica. Ryan and I didn't used to be friends, in fact we used to hate each other. In kindergarten I think the nicest thing I did to him was knock down anything he was building and the nicest thing he ever did to me was take my lunch bag and throw it on the floor. But we started to get close at the beginning of third grade. Actually, I don't know how we even get along. We both have so much charisma, we try to take over each other. I think we used to play together much more last year than we do now. He lives a much faster life than I do, and we aren't so interested in the same things. He hates chess, for instance, and he hates competitiveness. So now we're giving up time for each other because we've kind of been separated. He's giving up his time with the popular kids and I'm giving up my chess time so we can play together. Usually we spend the first hour arguing about what we're going to do.

Jessica is really, really sweet. I've known her since before I got sick. She's just plain really nice. When she comes over we mostly play on the computer. The thing about Jessica is she doesn't give in to things really easily, but if you want something, like if you want her to draw you a picture — she's really good with art — she'll do it. She used to be the biggest blabbermouth in the grade, but now she's the second biggest blabbermouth. I'm the first. But you might have been able to tell that by now.

I also have some good friends from camp. My first year at camp, I wrote this poem for Tina Kenney. I was seven and she was fifteen:

I will
Sing Life

The Way You Change Things

If I am alone
There is a clear and empty
Blank sky.
If I am with you I see blinking, shining, beautiful
Stars in my heart.

When I am alone
In the forest
I see only woods
But when I am with you I see nature.

Last night you looked like a dancing violet in the wind.

I don't really have any good friends who are amputees. It would be sort of nice — I wouldn't have to try to keep up with them all the time — but on the other hand, sometimes I like to be really active and try to keep up with people. It stretches my limits and gets me to do more.

As far as enemies, I'd rather have enemies who are amputees, because they wouldn't bug me. Or like at camp, where nobody is going to bother you about something because you could just as easily bother them back about something. I have an enemy on the bus. He's a pain. He's very big for a second grader. I wish he was smaller so if he started to bug me I could stand right in front of him and say, "What were you saying, twerp head?" He says really stupid things like "You use conditioner in your hair." Using conditioner for a boy is not exactly considered cool. Or he'll whisper to another kid as loud as he possibly can, "How about we chop off his head and go bowling with it?" Or he'll say something about my scars, like "Adam's got huge pimples all over his face." Really stupid things.

Some people stare at me. It doesn't really bother me. I mean, I'd rather a kid just came up and asked me, but it doesn't really bother me. I just think to myself, "If this hadn't happened to me and I saw someone else, would I stare?" They're just curious. Sometimes if I see someone who has a really different situation, I stare, too.

MY family is really great. We just got back from a trip to Las Vegas and we do all kinds of things together. My favorite vacation was in Vermont. It was a really big ski house and we'd all huddle around the fire together and drink hot chocolate and we'd go places together. My mom is very comfort-

ing and calm. I like to talk or just watch TV with her. My dad understands, and he gives great advice. One thing that's really great about my dad is that he doesn't know as much about the law as I do. So once, I signed a contract with him, and since contracts with kids under eighteen don't stand up legally, he had to keep his part of the bargain — but me, no way.

They got a much better perspective on life from what happened to me. They learned to always get a second opinion and to be a lot more cautious when you're sick, and we all learned who our real friends really are. Our real friends stood there with us and our not-so-good friends would just say hi every once in a while.

My sister, Allison, is kind of a major pain, she's six and she basically drives me crazy. She always wants to be in my room, and when I tell her to go do her homework in Bolivia, she doesn't. I really don't like any of her friends, either, but when it's just me and her at home, we play together. She helps me with a lot of things, like getting stuff for me when I have my legs off. She gives me hugs when she's in a good mood, which is three times a week on average. She doesn't remember me from before I

I Will Sing Life

was sick, so she's used to it. When Allison grows up she's definitely going to be pretty: tall, thin, shoulder-length hair. She'll look nice. Underneath it all I guess I really do love her. Some of the time.

ANOTHER thing that I totally love to do is ski. I got started skiing last winter when my uncle became a volunteer ski instructor for a handicapped program in the Sierras. So I went to California and learned to ski there. I was there for two days and then last year and this year I went for a week of skiing with the 52 Association, which does all these great sports for handicapped people. Last year I heard about a ski race at Windham and found myself in it. I was the youngest kid there. I didn't do that well, but I still can't even believe I did it. I'd like to be in the Olympics for skiing.

I ski on my prosthetics and, actually, I'm very good for skiing because I have a habit of keeping my knees in and being a little bit hunched over when I walk, but that's the way skiers are supposed to keep their balance. I control the skis by shifting weight and using the binding on my right foot. Unfortunately, sometimes by sticking your binding into the ground you stick it too hard and it gets stuck in the snow and you're in trouble.

I still have trouble getting up on my skis. It's really, really hard because my arms aren't long enough to push me far enough up to stand. And there's a weird way of doing it on your stomach, I can kind of do that, but once when I did it I sprained my side.

I started out very nervous in skiing. Actually, I wasn't that nervous until I had to go downhill. Then I was like "Aaaaah! How do you stop?" I guess when I just approach new things, I'm nervous. When I first went to camp, I was too nervous to swim. I guess the reason why I just don't want to go in the water is probably that since I don't have legs or anything, I don't have security. If I fall, I'm in trouble. Dahlia asked me to swim with her every day. I told her I just wasn't too confident anymore. Then one day it was really really hot and everyone in camp was in the pool and I just decided I could do it. When I first got in, I was even more scared. For a while I just sat in the shallow end and then I put my arms around Dahlia's neck and kicked my legs and she dropped me and made me almost drown. But I was so excited about swimming that on my last day of camp I made her take me out at seven in the morning and the two of us were the only ones there because the water must have been minus forty degrees. The next year I made a bet with my counselor, Eric, that if he'd dive in the no-diving zone, I'd get into the water for a minute. That was good, because I told on him.

Conquering your fears is a big part of being able to do whatever you want to do. The first step is to understand exactly why the fear is there. The next step is to understand that maybe you have to have part of the fear, but maybe you can get rid of some of it. The next step is to try to destroy the root of it.

Like in the fear of swimming, the root of it was that I was afraid of water. So every once in a while I'd spray a little water in my face, then try bobbing my head under water, until I got used to it and was able to swim.

Or the first time I stood up on my prosthetics. I was scared that I was gonna fall, but then I calmed down, and I realized that if I fall, big deal, I fall. My motivation was high because I knew what it was like and I wanted to do it again. Before, I was taking advantage of being able to walk, and when I lost it I was so sad. But when I finally stood up and walked, it was so exciting. It was like I was doing it for the very first time.

When the Tree Stands Up

When the tree stands up
And its heart feels good
The other trees ask, "Why are you happy?
We're just wood."

"Before I was on the ground.
I grabbed onto a rope of clouds
And was pulled up.
A vine bandaged up my roots,
The sun sprinkled me with pines that are green all year round.
I felt like being born —
Like being there again for the first time.

Before I saw only my bed of darkness,
Now I have owl's eyes.
Before I smelled sushi-smelling worms,
Now I smell fresh air like the sticky stuff inside of pine cones.
Before I heard seeds closing up, like squirrels hitting leaves.
Now I hear budding chirps.

Before I had cold cups of memories,
Now I have holidays of green.

I am an arm of nature.
My branches are the fingers of the forest,
Stroking memories of the very first Spring."

Tina Kenney

TINA SPURNS the stereotype of sick children who smile sweet, brave smiles as they fade passively into their armchairs: "People expect that just 'cause you're sick you've got to be some kind of angel. Ha! Sophomore year I don't remember a day I didn't get detention." Tina can be tough, especially when she feels that people's expectations are interfering with her determination to be herself. Yet, when she is most herself, she is also tender. She spent some of those defiant sophomore detentions writing poetry.

Diagnosed three years ago with a rare and aggressive primitive neuralectodermal tumor in her jaw, Tina was told by her doctor that she might have only a few weeks to live. She and her mother made a list of all the experiences she wanted to have before she died. Tina soon realized, "If you put enough stuff on the list, you can't die, you just won't have time." Their list was filled with ski trips, shopping sprees, vacations, movies, and parties. As the list grew, the tumor started to shrink. A remission, a relapse, and then another remission later, bungee jumping has just been added to the list.

Even in the hospital, Tina had to squeeze chemotherapy into her busy schedule. As soon as she was strong enough, she would scramble from visiting with friends on the ward, to gossiping with the nurses, to playing with the babies. Then, oblivious to the monitors and intravenous lines surrounding her, she would phone her school friends and counsel them through their teenage love lives, with her characteristic blend of tender and tough, "But honey, you're being an idiot . . ."

When Tina is out of the hospital, she tries hard to be just another teenager in ripped jeans who hates school and loves her boyfriend. However, typical teenage carelessness is difficult for Tina; she is aware of her uncertain future. She spends hours at her "thinking spot" on a lake near

I Will Sing Life

her house. She writes poems there and at night she names the stars after close friends who have died.

The night sky is not distant or cold to Tina. It is full of the life that her friends never got to finish. When Tina talks tough, the stars named Rex, Erin, and Meredith lend her their fire, and in her more tender poems, she sees from their high and sparkling perspective.

Her chapter has been compiled as a scrapbook of the sort of thoughts, memories, and poetry that keep her company in her thinking spot. The scrapbook is a means of rebelling against a systematic world of doctors and pill schedules, classes and detentions. She wanted it organized according to the same basic principles as her bedroom: "It *is* organized, *I* can find everything. My clean clothes are on the floor and my dirty clothes are on the floor. That way, if I need clothes, I look on the floor."

A Day in the Life

I wake up every morning
I get up, take a shower,
Throw on some clothes
Tromp downstairs
And grab that everlasting cup of coffee,
Stare up at the nasty clock and give a nasty sigh.
It's time to go.
I jump in the car,
Pick up Stacy who lives out in the middle of nowhere,
But no one likes to drive to school alone.
I mope between the buses
And read that "afterschool soccer is canceled today because the field
     is flooded."
What? it hasn't rained in three days.
The bell rings,
I kick my locker, as the rest slam one by one and the last of the
     students graze into class.
I arrived early to school but I'm still late to class.
I go to classes I like,
I sleep through classes I don't.
Was that you I bumped in the hallway?
I don't go along with the dress code,
And by the way, I have cancer.

At school last week, everyone was sitting around combing their hair.
All day it's "Oh, do my hair, braid my hair, I'm going to color my hair,

should I perm my hair? Who's got a brush? Who's got hairspray?" So I just pulled out my lotion and started rubbing it into my scalp. I still feel uncomfortable about not wearing my bandanna around certain people. Because you still feel the wind and it makes you feel bald.

It's cool to be different. I mean, I've always liked throwing a monkey wrench into everything. I think it's really funny to be obnoxious in places where they expect you to behave. When I go out, I'll get dressed up all weird and not wear my bandanna just to see what people will say. Little kids don't know better, so I don't have a problem with them, but I do with their parents, who say: "Don't stare, don't stare" and then turn around themselves. I've heard people say, "She's a druggie, she's a skinhead, she shaved her head on purpose." Total strangers, in supermarkets.

I've walked right up to them: "Do you have any right to say that about me? You never seen a bald person before?" I say, "I'm studying teaching at Tri-County. I get A's in school. I don't drink, I don't smoke, I drive my mother grocery shopping. And you don't know anything about me and I've got cancer." And then they're, like, "I'm so sorry." Well, I don't need

the stuff you've been saying behind my back. I'm much more comfortable when people come right up to me and say, "Excuse me, I'm curious, why don't you have any hair?" The other day, perfect example, we're sitting in the library cracking jokes, and this kid came in and had a big spot of hair missing, and we were all "Did he get shot or something?," starting all these rumors. And I'm, like, "I'm gonna go ask him." He was happier that I asked him that, than sitting there being made fun of for the whole period. Hey, if I say people should come up to me and ask me, that's what I'm going to do to them.

To Whom It May Concern,

Staring at me won't help. Talking behind my back, too scared to ask what's wrong, hurts more than it helps. Avoiding the subject when I'm around can make a person feel left out.

I know you are scared for yourself. Once you see it happen to someone, I know you fear for yourself.

I Will Sing Life

The best thing you can do for me is don't avoid me. I don't bite. Treat me like your friend. Don't tell me how to get well — I have experts for that. Just let me be me. Not a poster child for your fears. Just let me be seventeen once again.

Love,
Tina

School is terrific. I'm a junior at Tri-County Vocational High School, in the Childcare program. I love going to school in the morning and shocking the hell out of people. Rumors get around when I'm in the hospital that I'm dead or dying or something, and then I walk into school and people are, like, "Oh my God," like they've seen a ghost or something.

I miss so much school that it's almost impossible to catch up. Including the time I spend at the clinic and in chemo, I miss fifteen or twenty days a month. I go in for a week of chemo every third week. Then I go home and then I go to clinic on Tuesday, and then most of the time I end up coming back Thursday or Friday for a blood transfusion. The next week I go to the clinic Tuesday, and then back Thursday or Friday for a transfusion, and then I go in for chemo again the next week. That's about fourteen school days a month. When I get back to school, there's always a test on something I missed. And when I finally get sort of caught up, I have to start chemo again. It's real important for me to stay caught up, so I work hard. I don't want to lose the year. But how are you supposed to graduate like that? So school is really tough. I guess I get through it like most other kids, with a lot of coffee and my friends and my boyfriend.

IT was really cool, my school did this benefit for me. I felt really bad at first, like it was just charity. They were just giving it to me and I didn't really need it, but then it turned out that I really did need it and it went toward the hospital and it really helped out a lot and I was surprised because I didn't think anyone would really come.

THE friends I have right now are better than the ones I had when I first got sick. I'm much more comfortable with the people I'm with now. Like Mel, you ought to meet Mel, she's really funny. It was raining one day and she wanted me to come out and I was saying, "I don't wanna come out. It's raining, I don't wanna get wet."

"Don't worry. My blow-dryer's here, you can use it when you get here," she said, not even thinking, and then, "Oh my God, Tina, I totally forgot!" I think that's great, because it means she doesn't feel uncom-

fortable or anything. When you're uncomfortable about it, you're always thinking, "I won't say anything about your hair."

I have another group of friends, my friends from the hospital and the clinic who have cancer, too. There's a support group for teenagers at the Jimmy Fund where we can talk. It's great because they know what's going on. I can sit down and talk with them and they know exactly what I'm talking about and I don't have to explain what a CAT scan is, and what it does, and *then* finish my sentence. It's a lot easier to be closer with them. I guess when you share the same life-threatening illness, you tend to get close. It is harder sometimes, especially when a person isn't getting better and I am. I feel really guilty, I guess. He's getting worse and I'm getting a lot better. I try to stay with them and I try to help them as much as I can. It was hard when I went into remission, because I wanted to stay in touch with them. I want to go into clinic and visit everybody and do what I can and I want to keep my friends from the hospital, but as I get better I just want to leave it all there. But I feel like to leave it all there I have to leave everybody that I know.

The tears on my face don't fall for sadness,
They fall for love.
Time spent together, we all became one.
When one is split, that one is no longer whole.
It becomes separate parts, one of dreams, one of memories.
The dreams encourage all of us to go on.
The memories keep us all together.

Then there's my boyfriend, Chris. First of all, he's totally comfortable with it. He's gotta be, well, let's just say, the most incredible person in the world. He's really supportive and it scares him sometimes when he sees some of my friends in the hospital and he knows they're not going to make it and he kind of looks at me and says, "Don't worry, kid, you're gonna be all right." Sometimes he doesn't even have to say it. Going out with someone with cancer has taught him a lot. He's learned how much you can really love someone and be afraid to lose them. He's learned to fight for me when I wanted to give up. Yeah, we have our normal boyfriend-girlfriend fights like everybody does, but I just love him so much and he draws so many things for me, especially roses, and he just loves me and I love him. Hopefully, someday we're going to get married.

You know how people say, you can't catch anything from anybody else? I think I've caught Italian from Chris. I never used to eat a lot of Ital-

ian food, but now I do because Chris is really Italian. I think I'm having Italian seep into me because his whole family is Italian and it's just so romantic sometimes.

> Wind that blows creeps into my heart,
>   like that of a dove touching water.
> Sometimes the coolness of the pond
>   brings shivers of relief.
> Then others it brings
>   reflections of sorrow.
> Love brings these things to me.

The main thing to do in Franklin is to hang out, drive around, do the "Franklin 500." It starts at McDonald's and ends at the new mall. It gives us something to do. We just drive around and find out who's where and what's happening. Everybody sits in the parking lot at Ames, people we know, seniors that graduated. There's a little market where everyone goes in the morning, gets coffee, kind of sits there and mopes until they go to school. Some of my friends are, like, "Oh, let's go try to get drugs" and all this. And it's weird, I've got so many drugs that I could make hundreds of dollars on the pills I've got in my house. I think the whole thing about doing drugs is the experience of trying to get them.

I REMEMBER when I was normal, before I got sick, walking along this road in the rain with Tommy, a really good friend of mine for a long time. I went over to his house one day and we were just having fun being friends and we went out for this walk around his neighborhood and it started pouring rain. And I was, like, "Oh my God, no. My hair's gonna get wet!" and he said, "Oh forget it," so we just kept walking in the rain up to this old warehouse and we just sat there and hung out and we were just being kids, drenching wet and talking and stuff. It was just one of those times when you don't really think anything of it, and now I look back when it rains, or I'm in that neighborhood and it's, "Whoa. That was a long time ago." That is when I really feel like my life has changed. When I was younger and hanging around with Tommy and my friends and everything, I never thought of growing up and being sick, or the possibility of not growing up. I mean, it was just a regular kid thing: grow up — live forever — everybody's perfect and nobody gets sick — only the bad people die — kind of thing. I mean, I was young, and naive, but I was happy. I

didn't have to worry about being sick or worry about who was sick or who was sicker than I was and going to the hospital and how I was going to get there or anything. It just didn't matter.

When you're sick, you get to do all these great things like getting Red Sox tickets. I know I wouldn't be going unless I was sick. Red Sox tickets are expensive. The circus, and Florida twice. I would never have gone to California. So it all kind of revolves around me being sick, and if I wasn't, I wouldn't be getting it. I'm happy that I did because it kind of gives you a break, like camp does. Something to look forward to. You think, "I can get through this last treatment, I can get through this last scan," and you just do it. But there's something false, something artificial about it. It's like you're doing it because of other people's generosity and not because of anything you did. You can't just be yourself anymore.

I hope when I get well it will be better, I'll be able to go back to feeling like I can just be myself. But once you've lived through something that is life or death like this, some things are going to seem trivial. And you never lose that. Every time I walk into McDonald's I see the thing for Ronald McDonald House and I throw all my change in there. Because I know what it does. I know if it wasn't for that, some people wouldn't be here now. You see a commercial for certain hospitals, or commercials about kids with cancer, and you can forget to an extent, and then you get kind of a reality thing, like, "Hey, this happened to *you,* don't forget about it." So you can't get away and there's always going to be somebody reminding you. Like, teachers at school will say: "Well, Tina, you're looking a lot better, you're looking really good," and I'm like, "Thanks," but they don't say this to anybody else.

I LIKE teaching, though. I teach little kids during the day. Sometimes they get really, really bad, they run up and put paint on me and I get so frustrated. Then I look down at their little faces and all I can think is "Gee, they seem so helpless and innocent, they don't have anything to worry about." Then when I have to go into the clinic, I look at the little babies' faces and they all look like they know what's going on. So I love teaching the kids at my school because they have no clue about life and they're just so happy. Their little smiles say to me, "Don't worry, Tina, it's gonna be all right."

Sometimes, playing with kids all day, I think, "Oh, I can't wait till I have my own kids." But then I think: "Well, wait a minute. What if I can't?" They say that I might not be able to. They can't ever be positive, but they said that there would be some high risks of the child having cancer and there would be a lot of risk for me because the tumor was on my hip and stuff like that. But they can't tell definitely. And I think about that kind of stuff and it's like, well, hopefully I'm going to be working with kids my whole life, someplace where kids need me and then they'll be my kids. But then I feel like someday I'm going to want to have a baby. You know, settle down, have a life, whatever . . .

MOST of my friends have jobs but I can't work. I've signed quite a few petitions for people who have been discriminated against at work because they've had cancer. There are places that won't hire me because I'm sick. As a high school junior, you need money, you need stuff like that. But I can't work. I'm in the hospital every two weeks and when I'm not in the hospital, at a workplace there's just too much chance of getting sicker. I won't even be able to work for a while after I get off treatment 'cause when you go off treatment, everything that you worried about before gets worse. When you get the flu when you're off treatment, you automatically expect you've relapsed. You bruise your leg when you're on treatment, you say, "Stupid bruise." You bruise your leg when you're off treatment, you say, "Oh my God, take me to the hospital." Everything is more intensified.

On chemo, you get through by telling yourself, "I need this to be alive." Then when you're off chemo, suddenly it's, like, "Well, what do I need to live now?" It's scary, not being able to go in the hospital anymore. Everything changes. In my case, there's still a tumor in my hip but no more cells. So we'll wait and see, I might need surgery or it might start shrinking by itself.

I LOVE karate. Karate's my favorite sport. I would do it all the time but I just can't train lately because I get really sick. Karate is wicked, wicked cool. I was always really shy until I went into karate. In the sixth grade, I was afraid of my own shadow, and people used to beat up on me. Then I took karate, and they beat up on me a little more just to see if I could take it, and I did take it, I never fought back. My teacher, Mr. Duffy, has to be the strongest man I have ever known. He has had multiple tumors all over his body for the whole time I've known him. I picture him as a stone statue that nothing can hurt. It will rain and snow and hurricane and blow, but he'll always be standing. That's his approach to everything. I thank him

I Will Sing Life

and karate for teaching me about strength and self-respect. Everybody needs that point in their life when they buckle down and say, "Hey, this is the way it's gonna *be*." You figure that out and you're a tougher person for it.

Limbs

The trees begin to dance,
with every gust of wind
you hear them sing.

They cheer on how glad they are
to be here.
The cracking and snapping are
not cries but excitement bursting
within themselves.

About two years ago, when I was in remission, I wrote a story of what I had been through with my cancer. This is the part about when I first got diagnosed:

It was the week before Christmas and all of a sudden I had a huge lump on the side of my face. At first my mom was cool. She said, "What do you have in your mouth?" Then she freaked right out. I got sent to an ear, nose, and throat doctor. He was an old guy but he was nice; he looked at me and poked around. Then he said that I had some kind of mass on my face. I said, "No shit." Then he said that I should have an M.R.I. done so he can see what it was. So we drove to this place. Then a nice nurse called my name and I went into this room to see a video on what was going to happen to me. It was pretty scary, but I didn't say a thing. I wanted to act like it was nothing, but it was not. Then I went into this big room and it had big steel doors and was steel plated. I got on this long table and it moved. The whole X ray took about one hour. Then we went to McDonald's. Then we drove home.

The next day I went to see another doctor. I was not scared until my mom said he was a cancer and tumor doctor. He looked at me and said that I would need some surgery. I got really scared. He said that it would only be an overnight thing. Well, I was there for a week. They had to run some tests on me. It was a lot of fun at first. But then on Wednesday a girl doctor came to see me. She said she had the results from my surgery and then she looked really weird. She said that she was really sorry but the results are not good. She said that it was cancer. . . .

When Lindsay, my new doctor, told me, " You've got cancer," I was, like, "No." She said, "Don't worry, we've caught it early, it's gonna be all right, we'll get you into remission. I'm determined that we will," and the first thing I asked was, "Am I gonna lose my hair?" She explained chemotherapy and she said, "Do you have any questions?" and I said, "Am I gonna lose my hair?" And that's when I cried. Not when she said I had cancer, not when she said I had to go in for chemo every week, not when she said I had to have surgery, and not when she said I had to have radiation. I cried when she said I was going to lose my hair. Trivial. The least of my worries now. I thought, "No, people like me don't get cancer, it's just those people that deserve cancer." I used to believe that was true.

I SAT in the hospital for a week. It took me three days to realize that they told me I had cancer. And it took me another week to even think about the thought that I might someday die. They said probably three months,

I Will Sing Life

tops. Because my tumor had gone from the size of a seed of a prune to the size of a tennis ball in six hours. And that's how it began.

> From a desolate island the lonely person
> peers into the forest.
> Knowing that on all sides
> he is surrounded by a body of water.
> Noticing the wild nature life
> that has been untouched by man for many years
> Knowing that now that man is here it will no longer be desolate.

I went through regular treatment, and it seemed like forever but finally, I went into remission and I felt like a normal person again. Everyone else in the sick world was in another world and I was me again. I'd have dreams about relapsing but I'd wake up and know that they were just dreams and they'd never come true. I started picking up where I left off. Then when I did relapse I figured, "Oh God, this is it. This is the end."

The first thing I thought was, "Mom, I don't want to do this anymore. I'm not doing it anymore. I just went through a year of this." I had worked out at karate that week really hard for a competition that was coming up and to get my brown belt. I had been really sore, just like the tumor on my jaw, a little bit of swelling, but I figured it was from karate. By that night, if I even moved or coughed, it was excruciating. Finally at around 12:30, when I'd been screaming all night, they took me to the hospital.

The doctors, I guess it wasn't their fault, but they made me feel like I was making it up. They kept saying, "Tina, we took an X ray and we can't see anything," and they said, "Where does it hurt?" and they would touch it and I would say, "No, it's in there, it's *in the bone*," and they said, "There's nothing." I've never been so demanding and horrible with doctors, but I kept saying, "It's in my hip, it's *in there*." I had a CAT scan, I had X rays, I must have had twelve doctors come see me that night. They thought I was exaggerating. They asked me if I was pregnant! Finally, at maybe five o'clock in the morning, they had this orthopedic specialist come in. He just touched me, looked at my mother, and said, "That's in the bone." Jesus Christ, I've been waiting for this guy for hours! He said, "You get her upstairs, admit her." And they admitted me.

I had an M.R.I. the next morning. Then when they told me I had relapsed, I was all by myself in the hospital, alone. The doctors came and I kept thinking: "I didn't relapse. It was just a bone spasm or something." The doctors weren't supposed to tell me, even if I asked, without my par-

*Tina
Kenney*

ents there to support me. But they did. They said, "We've found another tumor — you've relapsed." All I remember is the feeling that I must have done something wrong when I was in remission: I didn't take a pill, I didn't go to church, I was failing at school. I should have known.

My mother came in with my sister, Beth, and Chris and I told them, "I relapsed. I've got another tumor." Chris couldn't deal with it. He left the hospital and started slamming his car around. He doesn't handle things like that well. My mother just collapsed, and my sister ran out of the room crying. Luckily, I had told Eileen the play therapist to come down because my sister wasn't going to handle it, so she was waiting right there for Beth and looked after her. My friend's mom took my mother out for a walk and smoked, my mom said, a carton and a half of cigarettes.

I Will Sing Life

Suddenly, I was on monitors and oxygen and I was just, "That's it, I'm gonna die." I gave up basically, and you get even sicker when you give up, but it was really close. And my friends were visiting and I could just see it, my friends won't even remember me as going out and having fun. They'll remember seeing me in the hospital, all these machines hooked up and heart monitors. And that's not the way you want to be remembered.

SOMETIMES I think doctors are just in it for their own self-esteem. They treat you like a test in school. If they cure you, they're good doctors. Lindsay, my doctor from Dana Farber, is great, though. She's always been really honest with me. You can't be just "Oh you're going to get better" if somebody's not going to get better. I think my guidelines for a doctor would be: make sure you tell the truth; make sure no matter how old the patient is, they've got someone with them to handle it; tell them all aspects of what's going on; show them all their X rays and surgery results, anything they want to know. You tell them straight and truthfully; try to be optimistic, but you can't lie and you can't joke about it — it's something very serious.

IT'S very hard to be on chemo. Chemo doesn't discriminate. It kills good cells and bad cells, whatever gets in its way. That's why it kills your hair and skin and fingernail cells and breaks down your immune system. Then you get infections and terrible mouth sores from things that wouldn't normally affect you. And the chemo is so strong, it's like drinking. So you throw up because your system doesn't agree with it; it's not supposed to agree with it. When I'm in the hospital, because I have the portacath and the needle in the whole week I'm there, I can't shower and I feel *bleaaah*. So I wash up all the time, wash my feet. Use smelly soap and lots of perfumes. A lot of deodorant. And then pray that no one comes in to visit. The other people in the hospital won't say anything to you because everybody there smells. We just all sit there smelling.

WHEN you're in the hospital, they decide when it's lunch, they decide when it's dinner, they decide when you go to bed, they decide when you get up . . . everything. And nobody ever asks anything, it's always "This is what we're gonna do. . . ." The nurses have this form you need to fill out every time you go in, with the exact same questions on it. You have to go visit everybody on the floor before you start throwing up, and they're asking questions: "Did you have mumps or measles or allergies . . . ?" Like you wouldn't have been in there if you'd had mumps since last month's

*Tina
Kenney*

visit. Then the infusion pump is beeping all night. If you have someone else with a beeping pump in your room, it sounds like a traffic jam in there. The pump beeps when your bag of medicine is empty, when there's a system malfunction, or if you move and pull your line a bit. It beeps seven to ten times a night and you have to call the nurse to fix it. Trying to sleep with those machines is like sitting in hell with a beeper.

The Lonely Time

The 7:30 shift walks slowly down the hall.
When I hear their voices I know
The lonely time has come once again.
Lights close their eyes, TVs hush their voices.
Mothers kiss their children good-bye.
The words are not said but heard, "I wish I could go home with
     you."
I know if the words were said, you would take me home.
Cries are not cried out loud but are understood, "I'm lonely."
The smell of the hospital comes back,
The gauze and the bactracin

I Will
Sing Life

The taste of Tylenol like a sour vitamin
The echo of doors and the chime of elevators
Remind me that I'm alone like the Miss Pacman in the playroom,
That stands there, always on, waiting for the patients.
I watch the traffic lights go from green, yellow, red
To flashing yellow like the light on the I.V. pump.
The night swallows me and I am alone with the night
Trying to dream of trees dancing spinning dances with bushes.

I told my mother I won't die in the hospital. I will never die in the hospital. Bring me home. She was, like, "I couldn't do it," and I said, "Just bring me home." And we have like an agreement, that if anything unforeseen happens to someone in the family, that person won't be kept alive on life support. Because we don't believe in machines. Pull the plug, bring me home. I've had a couple of friends go home to die. You say good-bye to them in the hospital and it's hard because you're saying good-bye not as in "I'll see you later," but "Have a nice afterlife."

Even once the doctors say there's nothing else to do, once they've

tried everything, you can never give up. I'd go to a faith healer if I had to. You can't just sit back and say, "My child is dying," and watch him play. That's torture. I'd drag him to every doctor and I'd bring him to church every day. Whatever I had to do to save his life, I'd do it. As long as you have something to look forward to at the end, there's a reason to just keep going. Like, when I first got sick it was, "We're gonna have a big party. We're going to go out to dinner in a limo." Just something to look forward to and to keep going for. Everyone says, "That's it. I've had it." Well, I'm going to California this summer, and I'm looking forward to the ski trip with the Jimmy Fund, and maybe to seeing the Red Sox. There's so much you've got to look forward to.

I CAN'T wait for prom. My dress is the coolest. It's black velvet with spaghetti straps and it's got purple kind of like paint squirts on the top of it and it's all tight fitting and it's purple on the bottom and goes on a slant, with a bow, and I'll have black nylons and purple shoes and a black bandanna with beads. It's gonna look really cool. I'm debating about whether to wear the gloves or not. I want to. I begged Lindsay to take my portacath out before the prom because the dress has a low neck and it will show, but I'm just going into remission and they want to wait to see if I relapse, which to me isn't being hopeful.

I don't know what I'm doing after prom. Usually everybody gets together and goes to the Cape for the weekend or goes out and goes camping or whatever, but my money's a little tight so I don't know what I'm going to do. But I want to do something really special for Chris because he's going into the army the next week and it's our last time to be together.

CAMP, sometimes people need it just to get away. And the counselors there know that. They know, "Hey, I'm not just coming here because I'm rich. I'm coming here because I need it. If I don't get away from the hospital, if I don't get away from all those doctors, I'm gonna go insane." After a week at camp, I think everybody improves. You go back to your doctors and they say, "Oh boy, you've got all this energy. Let's try some new tests." Then everything starts getting better.

I think camp is like a giant battery and they issue you a plug of friendship when you walk in the door and everyone gets recharged. Everybody cares. At first I thought, "Oh great, a nice mushy camp where everybody's hugging and kissing. It's gonna be stupid." But once I took hold of my plug and plugged in, everything got better. It felt like all my illnesses went away and I didn't get sick the whole time I was there and I didn't bleed. I didn't even have to get a transfusion.

The last few days of camp, everything gets real emotional and real intense. You say everything you have to say to each person, because you know that some people won't be back next year. But then, on the last day, you say, "See you next summer," real relaxed, to let everyone know you're pulling for them. My first year, Jeannie said it to me and I said, "Um, yeah, maybe," but it gave me that encouragement I needed to make it back there. Our parents tell us all year that they are pulling for us, but it helps to know that there's a whole camp of people pulling for you, too.

Sometimes I think about camp with snow all over the ground, no kids running around, and it really bothers me. I miss camp. I miss getting up in the morning, even if that stupid trumpet was blowing. I miss fighting over the shower with a whole bunch of girls, too. Most of all, I think I miss the togetherness it gave us. To spend that much time with people that you could relate to, just like high school or something, when everybody's the exact same.

Off on the wings of cold winter winds,
The sounds of splashing from the children in the pool disappear,
The cabins finally cleaned, and the meds finally stopped,
As the cars with the last counselors finally leave,
Camp starts its long wait in silence,
It will sit alone through the snow and the wind
Waiting to be awakened by the laughter of the children come
     summer.

MY family is really great. Sometimes they can act like a giant battery, too. A lot of times we fight. Beth and I don't seem to get along. We have an older-younger sister thing. I don't mean to pick on her, but I do. I really hate it because I love my sister so much and I really think she doesn't think I love her. But sometimes we just can't get along. Lately it's so hard because she feels like everyone's paying attention to me and I feel like everyone's paying attention to her. But a lot of times that happens with siblings. Hopefully, when I'm off treatment we'll get through this. I know we will.

Mom

Sitting up late talking,
Telling you my dreams and ambitions
To grow up and live.
Sometimes wanting to cry or wanting to laugh.
Hoping that by all my hints
You would find out all my misdoings.
Then forgive
Me without saying a word.
Knowing that at times I had lost your trust.
Thinking all the things I had done and never got caught.
Wanting to tell you my whole life but
Wondering if you would never forgive or just not understand.
No matter what I thought I love you till the end
Because you're my mother.

When I first got diagnosed, I didn't have time to think about myself; I helped my parents. My mom and dad are very different about it. My mom cries and yells and is always there. She's really given me a lot of her personality, she believes in being herself. She says: "If the world was meant to

I will Sing Life

be full of clones, God would have never invented striped underwear." My dad worries all the time but he tries not to show it. He had to get a second job to make enough money to pay all the medical bills.

I'm not home a lot when I'm out of the hospital, and that drives my parents crazy. It's real important for me to go out and party a lot because the whole time I was supposed to be going through all that teenage stuff I was in the hospital. I like spending a lot of time with my friends because I miss them and I'm afraid that everything's going to happen when I'm not there. I don't want them to forget me when I'm away for the week. I go out every night of the weekend, even though my parents try to stop me. Weeknights, too. Sometimes I go out even when I'm exhausted, so I won't miss anything. I worry what my friends will think if I leave early, so sometimes when I'm really tired, I'll call home and start yelling at my dad that I don't want to bring the car home NOW, and he'll play along and start yelling back that I have to or I'm grounded. It's not really lying, it's just a safe way that I can go home and rest.

> To the People Who Care,
> The ones who are there through the needles, surgery, and chemo.
> I thank you. You are the ones who keep me going. You are my shoulder to cry on and my punching bag to let my aggressions out on. You are the reason I put up with the pain.
> I give a second thanks to the people who look past my shining head and into my heart, past the scars to the friendship inside. I know these people inside are staring but don't let it out because they know that I am not just a cancer patient. Thank you again for letting me be me.
>
> *Love,*
> Tina

I've had so many transfusions since I've been sick, I've lost count. I love to imagine the different kinds of people who have given me blood and think about the ways they change my personality. I always wanted to know what that person did. What's their name? Where do they live?

My Transfusion Family

Tina Kenney

Forty people all thrown into one,
As the argument starts, I say, "It wasn't my fault, it was Bill the
    doctor, he wanted to remove the dog's kidney. I just did
    it."
I do things I would never have done before, things like crossing
    in the crosswalk. That comes from Ken the cop.
Russ the mechanic, who fixes fenders, needed some business so
    he made me hit the fence with the car on the way to
    school.
Then there's Krystle, who's short and loud and walks with her
    nose stuck to the ceiling and she makes me pick on little
    freshmen for being ugly because she has nothing better to
    do.
There's Joan, a kind little old lady who's eighty-six. She makes
    me bake cookies instead of going out on a Friday night. My
    friends don't like her.
And Brian the Big Brother who makes me pick on my little sis-
    ter. I push her down stairs and put Windex in her mac-
    aroni and cheese.
There's Anreaka the sex therapist who makes me light romantic
    candles for my boyfriend and cook great Italian meals.
    She's my favorite.
Then there are things that I do and don't know who they come
    from.
All my actions are from my transfusion family.
Even though it's pretty crowded in here, I'll probably be able to
    fit you in.

I never really go to church or anything. I would if I only had the
time. I know they say you can always make time for church, but I get out
of the hospital on Saturday, and by the time Sunday comes, I'm just so
tired and everything from being in the hospital. My father can't go because
he works all the time, my sister's got soccer games. I mean, I know it's a
sin or whatever to miss church, but I'm there in spirit.

I used to go to church a lot. But I was sitting in church one night — a
good friend of mine was dying of cancer, and I went to church to pray for

her. And I got into church and it was 10:02. There are certain things I'll always remember. They said, "Let's say a special prayer for her," and it turns out at that moment she passed away, which is really bizarre. And this different priest gets up and goes, "People who end up with cancer and stuff, it's because they didn't pray enough to God." Ever since that day, I haven't walked into a church.

He had no right to say that — he didn't know what he was talking about. It's an impact like that, that changes people for the rest of their life. I don't know if I'll ever . . . Sometimes I feel like I don't believe in God at all. It's like — if there was really a God and God's supposed to save everybody and forgive everybody for everything, why did He let me get sick? Why does He let two-year-olds, who never had anything in their life, die? Why doesn't He stop it? I mean, if anyone had to get sick, why couldn't it be somebody who deserved it? I always said nobody ever deserved it, but if there really is a God, why does He let that happen? I personally don't think there's one man, whether he's a spirit or a person, that can decide, "It's going to rain, it's going to snow," or whatever.

They said before that if I relapsed, I'd relapse within a year and I went a year and three months, so you just have to wait. I have this feeling it's going to happen again. I just can't see myself not being sick. You know how people can see themselves getting old and dying of old age? I see myself dying of cancer. Whether it's next year or twenty years from now. Maybe not. But after what I've been through, it's kind of the way it seems. Either that or dying because of all the medicines I had to take when I was on cancer maintenance. Liver dysfunctions and heart problems. It seems as though there are more disadvantages to going on chemo than there are advantages.

If I relapsed again, I would just . . . because of the fact that I know that I wouldn't get into remission again, I don't really know what I'd do. I'd be upset, I'd be really pissed off because I'm just starting to get my hair back. They say I have five-o'clock shadow twenty-four hours a day. Chris always says, "If you weren't here I'd kill myself" and all that. My parents say they wouldn't be able to handle it, but I think I'd keep trying because you can't just give up and not do anything. And I wonder what you do when you're dead. Ever see those movies when you float around and all this? I seriously wonder, I mean, what happens when you're dead? Do you fly around in the sky or do you just decay in a box? Are you dead or are you *dead*-dead? Imagine not being able to breathe, not having a heartbeat, not being able to be seen or anything? I just can't picture myself . . . I can't die because I just . . . I wouldn't look good dead. I'd look horrible. I went to the funeral of a good friend of ours, and — well, not to be rude and obnoxious, but — they were all, "Didn't he look good?" No, he looked dead. He looked white and he looked like he was lying in a box dead. I'd be a poltergeist. I'd love to sit in certain people's houses and listen to what they say: "Oh Tina, she's such a . . ." *BOOM,* I'd throw something. You wouldn't have to worry about money. But they say you don't eat or anything. I couldn't walk around and not eat cheeseburgers and pizza, I'm not eating flowers and salads!

I HAVE kind of like a thinking spot by the lake near my house where I like to go down and think, relax, look at the stars.

When my three friends died
I looked in the sky and saw their faces.
The sky had been empty before
And now it is full of their life.
They all look out for me.
As I watch out for them.
When I dance, the smallest star, Erin,
Watches me for her wish was to die dancing
And when she could not move anymore,
She wished to go to the ocean.
When the wind blows, the stars move and she dances
Over the ocean.
She moves to her own beat.
I dance to the beat of the world.
We dance as one.

When I cry, Meredith crinkles the tips of her star to
Make me happy, she used to shrug her shoulders and
Giggle just to make us laugh.
She quietly stays in the middle of the sky so she can
Watch everything go around her.
When her light shines dim, I smile to cheer her up.

Later at night, when my night grows dark,
There's a big tough star that's squishy in the middle,
Rex shines bright to light my way.
He used to say he wished he lived closer but now he
Sees me every night.

He still loves practical jokes.
When I had nothing to laugh about, he stole the moon
And put it in my backyard.

When my time comes, my star will be waiting with them.
They are building a brand-new star.
They beat on it to
Make it tough enough to hold my will.

When you've got a disease like mine, you can't not think about death.
You can't sit there and just: "Oh well, I'm gonna go on forever and . . ."
Like the other day in school, everybody was: "Oh I'm gonna get married,
I'm gonna have kids, I'm gonna do all this . . ." I just want to live to next
year. They say, "Don't worry, don't worry." Don't worry? I'd like you to
have a doctor tell you you've got cancer, that you've just relapsed, and
then hear you say, "Oh don't worry." I mean, yeah, I want to live, but I'm
not hoping for twenty years from now, I'm just more concerned with making it to next year. I just want to graduate. You've got to have goals for
yourself that are more than you can reach, but not something that you
know you can't. It's better that way.

Life picks flowers for a short time
Bringing them from glory and beauty
To a withering death.
Being beautiful for only a short time,
Knowing it is happy, at least for a short time,
It is willing to accept.

If I could have one wish in the world, it would be for peace and harmony. For everyone to just get along. Somehow, in the hospital, it didn't
matter if you were black or white or bald or fat or skinny or green. It
didn't even matter if you had scales. They would try to cure it. They would
never turn anyone away. People would come lumping in — is that a word?
Hopping in with one leg and they'd give them another one and they'd
walk out with pride. It just bothers me so much, people with prejudice.
"Don't go near that person, they've got AIDS!" I've known a couple of people with AIDS. God knows, I might have AIDS, you know, transfusions all
the time. Would all my friends do the same to me? Probably. It's the disease, not the person. I could walk up to my best friend and she would be
like: "Tina, I love you but I can't go near you anymore." It seems like everything is like that.

I always have this dream. Well, everybody says they never want to be discriminated against because they have cancer. I keep having this dream that when I grow up I create this place for kids with cancer and blood diseases. It's like a school and there's a big house with dorms and everybody gets their own room. We have a hospital there so they don't have to go to other hospitals, and there are recreational activities. I can just really see myself doing it. But then I think in a way it's separating them. Kind of segregating the world: people with cancer on this side, black people on this side, people with AIDS on that side. I think it's good that people with cancer get out into a community and let people know how it is.

But if I had a choice, a lot of the time I'd rather go live somewhere like that. I wouldn't have to pull this shit that I'm always doing here with my regular friends, none of this "have-to-be-macho" stuff and "you-gotta-fight" and all of that just to be cool. Because everybody would just be together.

Cherish love, joy and peace,
They may not always be ours to have.

P.S. I'm in remission again! My remission party was amazing. The band made the whole party. It was my cousin's band, and they set up in the middle of the kitchen! It was like imagining a hundred people stuffed in a little box. There were people there I didn't know because it was in the Franklin newspaper. A restaurant gave the food and the My One Wish Foundation helped organize it. This huge gorilla-gram showed up! It was incredible!

Pia Taylor

ON THE WAY BACK from dinner one night, Pia suggested to a group of campers and counselors, "Let's all start laughing for no reason at all, until we realize how silly we're being, and that makes us start really laughing." It worked, and Pia laughed the longest and hardest. She has become an expert at producing joy out of nowhere. For seventeen years, she has lived with a severe case of sickle cell anemia and with poverty, and yet she is most famous at camp for her stories that make people laugh.

Pia often contrasts her view of life with Tina's. While Tina rushes to fill each moment with activity, Pia tries to slow each moment down so that she can look around inside it. If she rushes, she might miss that perfect detail for one of her stories.

Once, when the rest of her cabin was playing kickball, Pia took a moment to lie down in a patch of dandelions. She explored them as eagerly, but much more patiently, than the bees buzzing around her. What she saw there found its way into the short story that closes her chapter.

Pia composed her short story orally and we transcribed it for her. Often, as she told it, her eyes would close and she would move with her main character, crouching when the character crouched, reaching out her hands when the character protected a flower from the rain. Her eyes opened only when the story made her laugh or when she would ask, doubtfully, "Is any of this good? Am I talking too much?"

A few days into telling the story, Pia went into an excruciating sickle cell crisis. A crisis is a recurring complication of sickle cell anemia. It occurs when the abnormal, sickle-shaped, red blood cells clog the blood vessels, causing damage and inflammation to the organs and tissues they should supply. For the week that she was in the hospital, her eyes rarely opened under the weight of a massive dose of morphine. She would try to work on her story, but it would be only a few seconds before she fell

I Will Sing Life

asleep or became incoherent. Most of the time, she would just hold our hands. Often she held them not so much because she needed us, but because she knew how helpless we felt.

Pia's short story is about a young girl and an elderly woman who notice a dandelion growing in a crack in the road. Pia talked about how the young girl resembles who she once was: "She cannot go to school, so when she is home or in the hospital, sick and lonely, she has a lot of time to think and to watch people." Pia also talked about how the flower represents who she is becoming: "Some people call a dandelion a weed, but to me it's a flower, it may be a cheap flower but it's a flower, and it's hell trying to squeeze up through that tiny crack with all those things trying to keep it down, but it's still prevailing, it's coming up out of there."

Pia knows that the life expectancy of people with sickle cell suggests that she will never reach the age of the wise, elderly woman. Yet Pia cares more about details that enrich life than statistics that limit it. Tucked in the last paragraph of her story is a seed floating over a patch of dandelions still in bloom, a detail through which Pia suggests that cherishing a complete life does not always require living a complete lifetime.

~~~~~~~~~~~~~~~~~~~~~~~~

I WAS nine years old and it was time for my oldest sister Debbie's prom. Debbie used to be my idol — I would take parts out of her personality and parts out of my mom's personality and try to put them together to make myself. I was up in my mom's bed because I had been in pain crisis for two days, but everyone was so caught up with the moment that I'm lying in bed with my legs hurting, and I'm screaming, "John, Stephen, come pick me up and bring me downstairs so I can see Debbie before she leaves." But they didn't hear me, so I said to myself, "Well, it's going to hurt to move but I am determined to see my big sister."

   I sucked in, clenched my teeth, and dropped off the bed, down to the floor. I wanted to cry, but I wanted to see her more, so I wouldn't let the pain take me over. I couldn't push off with my legs, so my arms pulled me, and then I pulled myself down the stairs headfirst. After I tumbled down the last three steps, my legs started shaking and my elbows were all burned up from the rug, and they were starting to sickle because they were holding all of my weight. So I sat there and I cried for a minute but then I said, "You have to go see Debra; you can cry after you see her." I crawled into the living room and there was my big sister with this bright smile and she came over and kissed me and all I did was just sit and look at her beauty. Her dress was a pastel purple and her hair was up and her boyfriend, Bam, had his tuxedo on. Ma was crying.

   After that, I said to myself, "I can do what I want to do in life, because I just crawled down these steps." It's going to hurt, but I'll get there. And what I know is, hey, I'm living in the ghetto, I'm black, female, poor, I have all those things against me and being sick is one more little thing added on. People are always telling me, "Go ahead and cry. You don't have to be strong all the time." What they don't know is that I don't know how to be weak. Unlike the people who were healthy and then happened to get sick later in life, I was born with this, and I grew up with a strong woman and her strength was instilled in me. So, it's a race, and unfortunately I have a few more hurdles to jump over than you, but I promise you I'll get there. It may take a few years, but I'll get there.

Ma is strong. When I look at a lot of the mothers that had children when they were that young, they're still sitting on welfare and I'm glad that she had the strength to say, "I want better for my kids." She went to college and she's a psychiatric social worker now. She had four kids when she was in college. She would be well-off now if she didn't have us all — in money she would. She's got nine kids and then there's about thirteen grandchildren, and we always had someone else in the house because they didn't have a family.

I grew up seeing that my sickness wasn't the worst possible thing that could happen. Where I've lived in New Haven, there was always somebody worse off. It's crazy around my way. It's scary, but you try not to think about that or else you'll be in the house your whole life. One night it was warm so I was sitting out on the porch observing things when Ma called me, "Pia, come upstairs and hang these clothes out on the line." I was mad. It was ten o'clock at night. Couldn't they wait until morning? But I went upstairs and I was hanging out the clothes and looking at the block. On the corner across the street from me there's three houses where they sell drugs. This lady, Anita, was out there with one of her girlfriends who had two toddlers in a carriage in front of her and they were talking to two boys and one of the boys had his arm around the other boy's shoulders. They're sniffing coke and smoking and I'm thinking, "Why do they have the kids out there watching them do their dirt? They're better off being left in the house, and that's dangerous enough." Not only that, but Anita's newborn is being ridden up and down the street by somebody on a ten-speed bike.

I heard a "boom" and I'm thinking, "The damn boys with their firecrackers." Then I hear "Boom, boom, boom, boom, boom," all in a row. That wasn't firecrackers!

I called 911 and my niece was running up and down the hall screaming, "Mommy, save me!" because even this four-year-old knew it wasn't firecrackers.

I ran down the front steps, and as soon as my foot hit the sidewalk everything was in slow motion. I could see that people were talking but I didn't hear any voices. My heart felt like it was going to pop out of me. I saw Anita clutching her chest and screaming the boy's name, but there wasn't any voice, and his friend was still standing with his arm around

where the boy used to be. I could see people hitting their fist into the palm of their hand and my sister Simone is hyperventilating because she went to school with this kid and I could hear Ma saying, "Oh, that boy is dead. He's dead." And I hear his friend saying, "We gotta find the No-Names." He meant he wanted to find the bullets to fill up his own gun. Bullets do not have a name until they hit someone.

This kid was sixteen, he'd only just had a birthday, and his blood was trickling down the sewer. When the ambulance came, if there was any chance, they would have started working on the kid right there, but they picked him up like a piece of meat, dropped him on that stretcher, and his arm was dragging on the ground while they were rolling it away. He's gone.

I started sickling in my chest, and my sister Simone is hysterical, screaming up and down the sidewalk, "Pia, I tell them to go to school, to stay in school."

"I know you do, Simone, but everybody has a choice and he knows how the street is, he did not choose to die, but he chose the street." A lot of people ask me, "Why don't *you* hang out on the street?" No! The street has nothing to offer. You may love the street, but the street does not love you. You might make some money selling, but it's a job with a terrible health plan.

From my experience with drugs for pain crises, I don't know what people get out of it. When I'm in the hospital, high on morphine, I'm not happy. I start hallucinating; I have side effects of itching and throwing up. Sometimes I want to say to the people who are sitting in the bathroom smoking their joints and cigarettes, "Do you want to come to the hospital and come onto my floor and see the babies that haven't done a thing to get what you are *trying* to get? Come here and let me show you what you are taking for granted. Not that I want to put on a show, but watch the kids who have tumors in their heads and the girl who can't express herself because her mouth won't move — her hair is gone and she can only move her left fingers. Give her the chance to have the gifts that you are taking for granted."

I FOUND out what sickle-cell was when I was five. I used to go to the program at Yale–New Haven Hospital and they left pamphlets around, and little by little Ma would tell me stuff. They used to have this doctor at Yale named Dr. Ritchie. To me, Dr. Ritchie was the world, and I used to get upset when he wasn't there and someone had to fill in for him. "Why isn't he here? Who said he could have the day off? I want to be sick when he is here." It made life better for me. I had to hurt, but, hey, look at this view I have to look at.

I remember looking up into Dr. Ritchie's face and I always had the misconception when I was little that white people couldn't breathe. Their nostril holes were so small. "They can't breathe. Ma, they're not breathing."

Ma used to try to shelter me from the bad things about sickle cell. I would wonder, "Why are you hiding this from me? I want to learn." One day I was eight and I was home by myself because I had a slight fever. I remembered that she had this folder that said "Sickle cell" on it, and I thought, "This is a great opportunity. She's always telling me not to look at it." So I started digging where she keeps her files and I saw stuff like teenage pregnancy pamphlets, lung cancer pamphlets, working mother files, and I finally got to the sickle cell file. I could imagine her with her finger pointing to it, saying, "Leave that alone — get out of it!" but I thought, "She lets me look at these pictures of a lady having a baby, which I'm not about to do, but she won't let me look in the file of the thing that I have.

Why does she have this in the house? Nobody else has sickle cell." I found this little pamphlet that said "Sickle cell," and it had characters that were bubbly-shaped like Casper the Ghost. It went through how you get it and what treatments there are, and it was easy to understand. But then I got to this other pamphlet that didn't have any bubble shapes on it. It was just plain and blunt. I started reading it — blah blah blah — until I got to the point where it said, "Most patients don't live past the age of twenty-five." I thought, "Ah, this doesn't pertain to me." And I flipped the page, but my eyes just kept seeing the words. I'd start the next line, but my brain wasn't saying it. My eyes were filling up with tears, and the blurrier it got, the faster my brain kept reading, until I closed that folder and walked over to my ma's closet. I sat there and I looked at myself in her full-length mirror and I started to cry. I started figuring out "How old am I now? I've got . . ." And then I realized that it means I could be dead *by* twenty-five. It doesn't necessarily mean I die on my twenty-fifth birthday. Ma was always telling me, "You need not know every single thing. It's not always good to know some things."

That evening, Ma was cooking spaghetti and I went up to her and I said, "Am I gonna die when I'm twenty-five?" She told me, "Don't worry about it. We're not going to worry about it because the day you start worrying about it is the day you die." She also told me that there are some people with sickle cell who live to be forty and fifty.

I used to sit and cry a lot because I didn't know what to expect. The support groups, you had to pay money to get there and get back, and if you're poor you have to buy the basic necessities first and see what you have left over. The questions in my mind were: Does it get better from here? Does it get worse? Can I get married? Can I have kids? Can I go to college?

I found out a lot when I did a paper on sickle cell in eighth grade. I scored an A+ because I got up there with my little chalk in my hands and I drew the little parents and their hemoglobin, and showed how you have a one-in-four chance of getting it if both your parents are carriers. It used to be that the only place you would find sickle cell was in Africa, but the slave trade spread it to Puerto Rico, Jamaica, Haiti, Cuba, and Panama, and then there are also people in Italy and Greece who carry the gene. The tribes in Africa gave it names like "Chwecheechwe" that sounded like a baby screaming, because the babies that had it cried all the time.

It's a blood disorder in which your red blood cells are shaped like a croissant. I always had trouble figuring out what I could compare it to because a lot of people don't know what a sickle is, so a croissant. When we get sick we call it a pain crisis. Your blood cells clog on top of each other, so you don't have any movement in your vessels. Whereas the normal donut cell is made to roll in the vessel, the little croissant just can't do that as well as the donut. Wherever that happens, it really, really hurts. It hurts a lot. I usually can't move and I have to go into the hospital, sometimes for as long as three months. They give me lots of I.V. fluids to get the cells flowing normally and they give me morphine for the pain.

A crisis happens if you get too excited, too emotional, too cold, too tired, don't get enough oxygen, get hit, even just having a common cold. The crisis can cause other complications, like a stroke, a heart attack, a brain attack. I used to be scared that I would have a crisis in my brain and be brain dead the rest of my life.

I told the class you shouldn't be scared of sickle cell because you can't catch it — you have to be born with it. You can kiss a person with sickle cell if you want, you can drink after the person, use the same spoon. People with sickle cell can get married and have kids, but it's probably smarter to adopt. Then I said, "All right, ask me a question. . . ." And the first question was, "Are you gonna be a doctor?"

I'm not like some people that are scared to tell other people what they have. Listen, this is me, I weigh 170 something, I have sickle cell, I'm from the ghetto. You want me? Fine. You don't want me? Too bad. I was living before I knew you and I'll go on living.

When I was little I wouldn't tell anybody what I had because once they heard the word *disease* I was no longer to be played with, talked to, or touched because they thought they could catch it. They used to pick on me and I'd go home and cry. I grew up thinking that I'd never be married or have a boyfriend because I had what I had, and that I was ugly because I had what I had.

Once in a while the teacher thought she was doing me a favor and would tell the class that I had a disease. Then it would be lunchtime, and we had to line up, and it was more like two lines and me, because the people who were in front of me walked five steps up, and the people who were in back walked five steps back.

Now I've wised up to say "disorder" because it doesn't leave as much of a print in your brain as "disease" does. When you think about it, it *is* a disorder. The cells aren't behaving correctly, you know? "You're out of order here, mister!"

I have more severe crises and I get them more often than most sicklers. The doctors don't know why. The crisis I had this winter, I had to

be in the hospital for two and a half months. The morphine they gave me for the pain stopped me from breathing and pneumonia got in there and my lung almost collapsed. I wanted to give up. I was tired of fighting. The worst part is having to rely on other people to do things that I want to be able to do, like going to the bathroom or brushing my teeth.

Most people with sickle cell get blood transfusion therapy so that the sickle cells can be replaced by normal cells, but since I became a Jehovah's Witness, I don't accept blood transfusions. It says "abstain from blood" in the Bible, so that means Jehovah's Witnesses don't eat blood or get it through an I.V.

We started becoming interested in Jehovah's Witness when I was eight. Ma had a friend from the office who was a Jehovah's Witness and she was mild tempered and Ma respected her and asked to go to Bible study with her, and then me and Simone got into it. Church for me and Simone used to be falling asleep and giggling, but at the Bible study group this lady taught us from *My Book of Bible Stories* and we loved it. In

I Will
Sing Life

school I was embarrassed that I couldn't read, but here they let me take my time in reading my little paragraph of the story, and that was one of the ways that I learned to read.

The doctors try to convince me to have transfusions. They say if I got them I wouldn't have this pain. When I had surgery, they really tried to convince me to get transfusions. They sat on chairs that were lower than mine so we could be face-to-face on my level and they said, "Pia, you don't have to do this. Regardless of what your mom says, the law says you do not have to do this." I said, "This is *my* choice."

January last year I was dying because I wound up getting fifth disease. My bone marrow stopped producing cells, and my blood count was low. It didn't feel like I was dying, but I was real tired and it hurt a lot. They said, "Honey, you're not doing too well, we need you to receive blood," but I said, "No." They called Ma up at her job and said, "We don't want you to take this personally because we like you, but we may have to take you to court because Pia is sick and she needs this blood." If it did come to the court demanding a transfusion, I would fight like I was being raped because that's what it is — I don't want this in my body. I told them that Jehovah would take care of things. Then it ran its course and I popped out and they said, "You have such faith." I said, "You guys need to have a little faith yourselves."

WHY should I worry about death now, when I've always had that question in my life? It's always a possibility. It's a possibility with anyone. I've lived my life for seventeen years and it's been wonderful. And if it's time, it's time, what can I do? Surgery is always dangerous for me because I don't take transfusions. Instead, they give me medication to make me produce more of my own red blood cells and they give me fluids and oxygen to replace what the blood would be doing. When I had my gall bladder taken out, it was weird because I woke up happy and I was wheeled into the operating room happy. It went through my head that there was a chance I would not see these people again, but I had a good life. I told Ma and my family I loved them and to trust in Jehovah and I'll see you in three hours.

I might have a hip replacement soon because I have vascular narcosis in my bones. That happens when you've had so many crises in a joint that the blood vessels break down and do not feed the bone. The hip replacement is dangerous because it's bloody, but I don't think it's the bloodiness of the surgery that's bothering me this time. It's because I've been able to experience a lot more life since I was fifteen. A lot of new things are opening up to me — I want to experience traveling without my family, going to college, romance, having a job. I couldn't see myself not being here. I guess once I'm dead I won't notice it, but what is scary is what I may be leaving behind.

A lot of people want to blame God for being sick. No. He doesn't choose you for these things. They're already here, okay? They are not God. And what are you going to do — "Oh, I hate God now"? It's whether you choose to have faith and believe or not, and I choose to. I don't ask the question "Why me?" about being sick, because there aren't any answers. It's funny, I ask the question "Why me?" about being fat, but the thing I should be asking "Why?" about, I don't.

I've learned to be strong about being sick, but sometimes I get low on my self-esteem. When I'm fighting sickle cell, it's just me against the disease. It doesn't talk back or react, but when I start thinking, "Am I pretty? Do I talk well enough? Do I talk too much? Is he going to like me?" there are reactions inside me. I get afraid that I'm doomed to have a man that sells drugs or a man that says, "You cook and clean and I go out partying and have all the women I want, and when I come home you better have the dinner on the table." I start thinking that I'm doomed to this G-H-E-T-T-O type of life. My brother used to be mean to me because I couldn't read and my younger sister Simone was reading the newspaper as a kindergartner. Nobody ever saw me; Simone was this beautiful kid with white teeth, and I was this sick kid with buck teeth who sucked her thumb all the time. Whenever they talked to me it was "How do you feel?" They never asked me to do stuff. My brother used to pick on me all the time, saying, "You're ugly" and this and that. I remember going up into my ma's closet where she had a mirror on the inside of the door and I'd close the door and I'd scratch my face. I kept scratching and scratching until it bled and I'd just sit in that closet crying for like two hours. I still get down on myself about the same things.

You've just got to find ways of coping. A lot of times I compare my life to other people's and I see that things can be worse. I might have to worry about where the next stick of butter is gonna come from, but then I think that compared to that man that's lying on the ground, I have a paradise. People say, "Don't you want to cry because you have sickle cell?" No! When I walk down the hall in the hospital, I don't take breathing for granted. I am thankful that I only have sickle cell, because once the little things go away I'm up and walking again.

Another thing I do to cope is observe the world. When the other kids are in school, I have a lot of time to think, and I try to figure out what I've made of my personality and who I am. Or when I'm lonely, I take a chair and sit by the window and just look at things. There doesn't need to be human activity. Just to sit and observe the way the trees, the leaves are blowing or how many dogs are going to go by this tree and pee on it. You know? I count those little things. What sidewalk has the most snow on it, or who shoveled their sidewalk the best, or who's done a lousy job? I observe things and see the outcomes. The other kids don't do that; they experience by making mistakes.

Observing also helps you have a sense of humor. Like, if someone's trying to be all secret, I'll notice it and I laugh and I tell them, "You're not doing such a good job of hiding it." I think it's from being poor and stuff — you just gotta laugh at it, there's no other thing to do. I'd rather be poor with a great sense of humor than poor and depressed because I'm poor. The few times we do have the luxury to go rent a video, we'll go get a comedy. 'Cause I want to keep laughing, you know. I want to be happy. Keep me laughing.

That's one of the daydreams I have, it's not exactly a good daydream. I've died and I'm in the casket and I'm ready to go to the funeral. And they're about to close the casket. And then I wake back up and say, "Wait a minute, wait a minute, I enjoyed life so much, I just gotta get one good laugh in. Just let me laugh one more time, please!" So they let me laugh — and then I die, lie back down on my pillow, and they close the door. I know it's bad to be dead, but it comes back to showing me that I had a good life. It was so good I just want to get my last laugh in.

I think that I daydream a lot more than the next person. I get a high off it. I can be walking down the street, my feet know where I'm going but my brain is too busy having a daydream. One is that we are in the city all by ourselves, and this guy is out to get me. And it's always me and my younger brothers and sisters and of course I have to be the heroine. "Pia, hurry up, hurry up, he's right there, he's right there!" And I'm saying all these things out loud and then I realize, "Stop daydreaming, you're out in public!" But once in a good while I have a nice one. You'll just see me sometimes when I'm sitting by myself, I'll be daydreaming, and all that time I have a smile from ear to ear. Ma's always asking, "What are you smiling about?" And I'll shake my head and go on back to what I was doing. I love those little things. To me that's living life.

My dad died when I was eleven. He had diabetes. There's many a day when Ma walks around the house saying, "I miss your father." I miss him, too, Ma. I daydream about him coming back, and it's always like the movies where I run to him and he picks me up and we're twirling in circles and then we kiss each other and then I slap him. And he says, "Why

did you do that?" And I say, "That's for leaving us and playing this trick."
And then he says, "Okay, honey, I'm sorry for doing that." And then he
comes home and gives me all the things I've been deprived of as a child.

Or I imagine that for my graduation present one of Dad's beneficiaries comes up to me and says, "Excuse me, are you Pia Taylor?"

"As a matter of fact, I am."

"Well, I have something for you, would you sign here?"

So I'm standing there, me and my prom date, and we're about to get
on the bus to go to the prom but he gives us a brand-new red convertible.
I don't know if I should make it a Cadillac or a Ferrari, I haven't figured
that out yet. And then he's also paid for my college and my living expenses. I have crazy dreams like that.

LOSING Dad before I got to know him is one of the things I find hard to
deal with. The older kids knew him and loved him. It seemed like whenever he did come by, I would be sick. He'd be taking the kids to the circus
and I'd say, "Dad, are you taking me?"

"Yeah, B-Baby," — that's what he called me — "come over here and give me some sugar." He had a nice beard and he knew that whenever my cheek would hit his I would giggle because that would tickle me. He held me there and I'd fall asleep, but whenever I woke up that bum was gone. He took off with the kids to the circus because he knew I was sick and couldn't go. Ma would always try to make things better. "We'll have some cake. The other kids aren't having cake." I'd be, like, "I'd rather go to the circus." Whenever they got to go out in the snow and play, I'd be sitting in the house crying.

But I miss Dad, he was a generous guy. One day he was mad at Ma, and he came in from New York and we were supposed to go to the toy store but it was closed, so he brought us to the pet store. He knew that Ma would be upset. Jolanda got two rabbits plus a bird, I got a bird, Candy got this big tank with a whole bunch of fish, Peter got a turtle, Eddie got two hamsters, and at that time two of my cousins were staying with us and he got pets for them, too. He dropped us all home and he didn't even set the stuff up. We were in the living room with the rabbits hopping around and the guinea pigs crapping all over the floor, and Ma walks in the house from work. "What is going on here? Why do we have this zoo in my living room?"

"Dad bought it for us."

She gets on the phone and starts screaming, "How am I going to take care of all these animals? I'm already having trouble feeding the kids." But eventually they all died off. We let the birds go so they could fly around the house, but my bird went up and dove into the TV screen, and then Jolanda's bird died from being lonely in the cage by himself. Peter cried when his turtle died. We buried it in the backyard.

FAMILY is another way of coping. We protect each other. I remember it was my first year being in middle school and we're walking across the schoolyard and about seven of these boys start coming and they circle around my brother and he's, like, "Go ahead, y'all, go to Ma's job." So I brought the little kids to the corner and I said, "Go ahead, go to Ma's job. We'll be right behind you, we just have to talk to our friends." Well, they weren't our friends. They were boys who didn't like Peter. Peter had to let this boy punch him because he knew that if he were to fight him and beat him up, the rest of the guys would jump on him. So I was watching this and I saw the boys talking about it and I saw them take out a knife. So I went and got a Jack Daniel's bottle from the guys who drink across the street, broke it off on the sidewalk, and said, "You guys might think that I'm crazy, and I'll be crazy, but one of you guys are gonna die today. I'll be

beat up, but in the four minutes it takes them to drive over here, you will bleed to death, so come on, who's gonna be the one?" And nobody wanted to get cut, so they left.

I was bad, I used to get into a lot of fights defending my sister Simone, too. There was this group of girls that didn't like me or Simone. I used to go into the bathroom during class when no one else was there and that group would have written on the wall about, "You be doing this, and you be doing that, and don't you be messing with my man," and I used to write things on the wall and sign it from one of the girls in the group. They wound up breaking up and fighting each other.

Simone takes care of me a lot when I'm in the hospital. She comes after school and then tries to rush home and have supper cooked for Ma. She comforts me, cleans my hair, brushes my teeth, but most of all she keeps me laughing. Usually I don't cry in the hospital, but last time there were people standing around and I was hurting, so I flipped over on my stomach to cry, and Simone walked in and kicked everybody else out of the room. She came and propped me up and held me and made me feel so much better. I was safer.

Ma holds my hand, and when she knows I'm hurting a lot she squeezes harder. Sometimes to take my mind off the pain, we'd play this game where she would have to follow how many times I squeezed, and then she would have to return it. She always knew when I needed to feel the warmth of her, and she would just touch me, and that's all I needed. I'd be able to smell her. It's Ma, and nobody else has that smell. She cried when I cried, but when she noticed I was watching, she would give me this bright smile with a tear running down her face. To distract me, she would tell me I'm making a beautiful park and it could have the craziest things in it. I'd put elephants walking around with lions' heads and it was always beautiful.

HAVING good friends can be the best part of life. When I was little, it always seemed I came into the hospital in the middle of the night and in the pediatric ward it would be dark, so I could never see this one girl's face, but I could hear her crying and I knew that we had the same thing because my mother and her mother would talk and Ma would always say, "We had a crisis" not "Pia had a crisis." *We* did have a crisis, because it affected the whole family. When the nurses prepared my room, I remember they parked my stretcher next to that other girl's and she would put out her hand and hold mine and she would say, "No matter how bad it gets, you always need to hold on, and hold on tight."

Years later, when I learned that she had died, I thought that I just want to do what she did for me, to be there for other kids. I'm not going to say anything like, "Oh, you're not gonna die." I don't know that. All I can do is tell them that while you're hurting, I'm here to help, and that when you're not hurting, we're going to live life.

MY first summer at camp, I got this beautiful feeling that camp was the girl who used to look after me in the hospital. Now that I'm a counselor, I get to help kids the way that she helped me.

My first summer, I remember I met my counselors, Mary-Ellen and Beth, and I thought they must be phony because it was like instant love — hugging and everything — and I didn't think anybody could just automatically love you like that, without ever seeing you before. Now I have that instant love thing, too. Now I know what real friends are. Other camps, no one wanted to deal with me. The other girls were able to run and jump and do everything while I was attached to the camp nurse. Here, I could be part of the closeness because everyone around me was sick, too. I got to participate, to act, and be silly.

And I got a chance to swim. I always wanted to swim. I remember
when I was nine, Ma took us to the beach and I went into my sister's
closet and I got out her sweatpants and her jeans and some shorts and
I said, "Ma, I'm going swimming."

"Oh no you're not. You're not going in there to get sick."

"Ma, I'm not going to get sick this time. I figured out a way so that
I wouldn't get wet."

She went back to cooking on the grill, and while she was doing that
I slipped away, grabbed my bag, changed my clothes, and I came out and
I was like the Puff Man, I had all these clothes on. I was determined to get
into that water, and I did. It wasn't long after that I got sick, but I had my
fun and it was worth it. Ma was upset when she saw me dripping wet and I
thought I was in for it, but all she did was shake her head and help me get
out of the wet clothes. I guess she knew it was hard. She tends to blame
what I have on herself.

When I first got to the Hole in the Wall Gang Camp I thought it
would be like another regular place where I wouldn't be able to swim and
I'd just be sitting there twiddling my thumbs. I remember them coaxing

me, saying that the water was heated enough for the kids with sickle cell, but I said, "I'm the one who's gonna be in pain for four days and you're gonna still be playing in the pool, so I have to choose wisely." While everyone was still talking to me, I was blocking them out. I was remembering when I would cry, saying that I wanted to go swimming and that I could have been the world's greatest swimmer and we might not know it because I'd never been able to get into a pool, and my mom would say, "Just be patient, Pia, all things may come in time." I'm remembering this and thinking, "You can't let this pass by you, this may be the chance to do what you've been wanting to do."

They put a life jacket on me, and I said, "Why do I need a life jacket? I'm not going in." But they put it on me anyway, and then I got in, and the water was warm. I *love* me some hot water. And I was just splashing and kicking and by the end of that session I kind of knew how to swim.

I used to think I'd never be able to have what normal people have, to do what normal people do. But once I got into that pool, there were alternatives. There are ways to fix things so that it will be possible for me. All it took was for someone to heat the pool enough so that I wouldn't have a crisis. I thought it would be asking too much for someone to do that.

I WANT to thank Paul Newman for that. I used to watch him on TV when I was little and I thought he was beautiful, but now it's not just his physical self and there's no screen between us. I remember him riding on this broke-down ten-speed up the road at camp and he was wearing these jeans that he had to have had since he was twenty. That's how old and raggedy they looked. He dresses like a poor man. I've only seen him in one kind of shirt and that's the gray sweatshirt, and he always has a white collar sticking out of it. He's not talkative. Joanne did most of the talking when they ate at our table, but he did joke about how tiny his legs were.

I WENT to the special session just for kids with sickle cell and I looked at the younger campers and I could remember when I was that little running around with sickle cell and all the fears I had. I would sit down with the older kids, and each person would try to describe what the pain of a crisis felt like. Somebody said it feels like a train is running over you, but then you wonder about that. How can you describe a train running over you if you've never been run over by a train? Or we'd ask: Have you had a stroke yet? Or have you ever had a pain in your brain? Has your gall bladder gone out? Have any of your joints been messed up yet? It was just nice

to hear those things. The great thing for me was to see the counselors with sickle cell and see that I can make it to adulthood, that people do grow up.

I fight hard all fall and winter so that I can have a summer of being a normal kid. And I keep those memories all year, because whenever I get upset or have to go into the hospital, I just get my photo-album and the tears are at the point where my eyes hurt and I'm just waiting for that first tear to just lap over my eye and run down my cheek. Then I take that picture out and those little awards that I won and that tear just flows over because I'm happy that I had all these things, I have had experiences.

When I was little, all I knew was the park, so I would try to imagine a park to distract me when I was sick. I didn't have any great memories that I could bring back and just want to live over. But with camp! You can sit back and just watch it and feel like you are doing it all over again and laugh when you should be laughing or cry. I've had the chance three times to experience the kind of love that a lot of people go through their lives not being able to experience. Once you step out of the car, this love embraces you, and you have no choice but to love back what's loving you.

There are a lot of places where I am the only black person, and I can feel it and notice it, because I've got to make sure I'm on my P's and Q's so I'll be different from the stereotypes. I did not realize until the last night, when we were going up to the banquet, and my counselors were behind me and I turned around to them and I said, "I cannot believe this, I'm the only black girl in my cabin."

They were rolling. "Pia, you're so cute, we love you to death. It's the last day and *now* you realize it."

I was, like, "No, this is great. I didn't feel this way. I was just me. I wasn't just the black girl in the cabin. I could be myself."

THE first year Ma said, "Pia, you need to write these kids because they may not be there when you get back next summer." And I said, "Pfff, they'll be there." I didn't write, but my friend Amy Fiske did and I was happy to get her letters. The second year the same girls ended up all in the same cabin again, so it was becoming a little family, and the youngest of us was Tami and I was the oldest. Amy was always there and had a smile. The second year I did write to Amy in September; she wrote me back saying happy birthday and stuff. Then I wrote her again, and it wasn't like Amy not to respond. Last year I was waiting to see everybody and be our little family again. All day I had been asking, "When's Amy coming?" and nobody would answer me. "Is she coming later tonight or tomorrow? Guys, what's the problem, is Amy sick? Is she not coming?" I never would have thought of the worst possibility. So Tami had me read this letter, and it's from Amy's sister, telling Tami that Amy had died. I was reading it and it felt like my heart was being crushed. This was the first time that I'd lost anybody from camp, and it hurt a lot because I didn't get to say good-bye or write her. It really hit me — some of us are dying here, it's not all fun and games.

I WAS glad to be a counselor-in-training last year and a junior counselor this year because I want to be able to give something back to the camp.

When I was a C.I.T., I asked Pete, who was probably nine, to the dance because he wasn't one of the popular kids in his cabin, and he's just kicking his legs because he's happy. The night of the dance I walk up to him, "Are you ready, honey?" And when I say, "Honey," he is so happy, he is shivering for happiness. And the other guys come over and say, "Pete, this is *your* girlfriend?" And I say, "Yeah, what's wrong with Pete? He's beautiful."

"How could you like Pete? Especially you, how old are you?"
I told them I was ten.
"Well then, why don't you want to go out with me?"
"Because I like Pete."
They were gaping and their fingers were stuck pointing at me and I was just happy, he grabbed my hand and we walked down the trail together.

I HAD a little girl in my cabin who would wet the bed, which is a problem for most sicklers because our kidneys cannot concentrate our urine. Because I know how it feels, I would wake up half an hour early, turn on the shower, and run her to the shower, and while she's washing I would wash down her bed with some ammonia and put the extra sheets on the bed and then get her back into bed and a few minutes later, I would wake the cabin.

Another girl was homesick and she had a crisis and I said to her, "Can you do me a favor? I'm looking for a park to go to."

"Yeah? What's in it?"

"It can have anything you want in it, and I want to go to this park because *you* made it."

She had lions jumping rope and licking lollipops, there were birds that were in a band, and I just started laughing because I could see a flamingo getting down with his skinny little legs and his wings out. I kissed her goodnight and I said, "Can you just lie here and think about your park? And before you know it, it'll be tomorrow."

I DON'T know if it's because I'm more mature than other kids, but outside of camp I don't have any friends my age. Most all my friends are older than I am. That's the way it's always been. The kids at school think either I dropped out or I'm going to have a baby.

I would have preferred for people to just come and ask, "Well, what is sickle cell?" In sixth grade everybody said I had AIDS. "Don't touch her!" We had Home Ec with the eighth-graders and I used to love this boy named Tyrell. Tyrell, oh, he was slammin'! I lived to go to Home Ec. And I would check him out from the corner of my eye while I made my little cake or whatever. And being a dummy, I told somebody I liked him and she ran and told one of the eighth-grade girls and they went and told him and then somebody out of my class told him that I had AIDS. And I said, "That's not what I have, jerk. I have sickle cell." And he said, "Well, what is that?" And he didn't want to be bothered with it. And when I got to high

I Will Sing Life

school, Tyrell wanted to come talk to me, and I said, "No, you had your chance, honey. I was a short little raggedy kid then, but you see what I turned out to be and now you want to come be my friend. You had your chance." I can understand the elementary or the sixth-grade kids, but he was in the eighth grade, he knew better. He just didn't want to find out. It shouldn't have mattered if I did have AIDS. He still should have talked to me.

I'm starting my senior year in high school this year, but I'm worried because I feel like I only have an eighth-grade education. I'm supposed to have homebound tutors when I'm sick, but they never send me my tutors so I've got big gaps in my education, but they keep passing me anyway. I'm just hoping that this year I can stay out of the hospital, unlike the past three years. I tell myself, "You don't miss school, you'll live without it," but where is my childhood going? There are so many things I'll miss, like being in the yearbook candid pictures, stupid things like that. I love to dance, but since I'm not in school, I can't learn the new dance steps, so Simone has to teach them to me.

The other day after school we went to the mall and hung out and laughed and joked, and other boys from other schools came by trying to flirt with us. I met up with Carlton, a boy we used to go to elementary school with. We joked about how bad Carlton used to be and how he would always wind up in the corner and nobody would ever have thought that he would turn out to be going to Notre Dame. And I said, "I want to shake your hand because I thought for sure you were going to be a future jailbird." And he started laughing. "I wasn't bad. I wasn't bad." It felt like I was a normal teenage girl for that day, the all-American little teenager, went to school, after that we shopped at the mall, had some cheese fries and our little drinks. Gossiping about people, talking about how slammin' our senior year is going to be.

I'VE come to realize that if I do die at twenty-five, life's going to be gone if I'm worried about dying. I love life too much to do that to myself. Even if I don't make it to twenty-five with all the bad things that have happened to me, I have lived a happy life. That's why that time I had fifth disease, it was like, "Hey, if this is dying, this is cool." I had this nonchalant attitude. This isn't hard. You just sit here. I wasn't afraid or scared. The doctors were scared. My mom was scared. I had this attitude that if it's time it's time. Although I might be dying young, I had a great fifteen years.

I look back at when I was in first grade, playing with crayons. I fixed

up the different colors so they'd be married and they'd build houses by me drawing a house with them. Then I'd go to the big box with the crayons that were too small and had been used so much that they had specks of other colors embedded in them, and those would be their kids. I can't believe how young I was then and how young I still am. And how much more I have to go. Yesterday Ma was in that little housedress and I was picking at her: "Ma, you gettin' old, you walking around in house-dresses now." She said, "You'll be amazed at how old I'll be with all the wrinkles on my face in the next twenty years." I can't think about the next twenty years. "Ma's forty-five?" We used to think that forty-five was eighty, and that eighteen was grown. I'm not grown. But life is going faster.

I guess my plans for the future *should* be different than kids who are healthy. They should be, but I don't let them be. I'm not going to live my life with the attitude that you never know when you're going to die so do everything now. I'm going through life trying to be as normal as possible. Normal people don't run from concert to concert doing fifty-eight states in a minute. I don't want to rush anything. I just want to experience having my driver's license in my pocket or college life. I want to take my SATs!

I want to take a moment to look at the sky, because if I don't, in a minute from now I may not be able to see it. I may not be dead, but something may make me go blind. I skip, and people laugh because there's a seventeen-year-old girl skipping along the street. I skip and I smile to myself because of the memories that I have had. I always try to make great memories because the bad ones are always going to stick, and the things that you would want to remember you don't, so I make it memorable, I'm passionate about it, even if it's just smelling a flower.

Exhale

I

Monet is wiping her face up and down on the pillowcase to sop the tears up because she is eleven and too old to cry. Just as she is about to fall asleep, the nurse walks in. "Monet, honey, I need you to turn around and blow on your spirometer."

"Do I have to?" She turns to look at the nurse, but the codeine is blurring her vision, she cannot see her eyebrows or eyelashes, just earrings and teeth.

"Yeah, honey, because if you don't do this your lungs will get weak and you'll get pneumonia."

The nurse pushes the button so that Monet's head comes up. "You have to do this ten times and then I'll leave you alone."

The first blow she doesn't even hear one ball cling to the top of the tube.

She inhales and breathes out her nose to prepare herself for the next deep breath, but she never gets more than one ball to hit the top.

The nurse turns out the light, tells her to sleep nicely and have good dreams and here's your call bell, and Monet hears the door close behind her.

II

Monet opens the door to her bedroom. The pain has not gone away, little movements hurt her, but she has a smile on her face because she is out, she is able to hear the sounds of her street again for the first time in a month. She has a lot of clothes on because she can't afford to get cold or it's back into the hospital. She drags a chair to the window and puts a shawl in the crack.

Across the street there is a white house, with an old Italian couple that lives there. The lady's name is Sophie. Monet doesn't know the hus- band's name, but she secretly calls him Herb. The old lady is out in her pink-and-white housedress with her little broom to sweep the sidewalk. She pauses and puts her weight onto the broom and her hand in a fist on her hip and looks around to see how beautiful the day will be and how far she has to go to finish her chore. When she realizes that she is daydream- ing, she starts sweeping again, getting every little cigarette butt, Cheese Doodle, and lollipop stick.

Monet is watching her broom and her eyes wander in the middle of the street between her house and Sophie's house. There is a skinny crack that opens into a little circle and then gets skinny again. There is grass growing up out of it and she watches the grass shake in the breeze, then she sees a tiny yellow speck. It could be a wad of yellow bubble gum or a banana flavored Now-or-Later.

III

A dandelion in the middle of the road? What's it doing trying to sprout up in all this activity? It will never have a chance. They are always having drag races on the street, pressing the gas and the brake so the wheels screech and smoke. Kids run up and down the street playing tag, Double Dutch, blowing off firecrackers, and down at the corner you have all the drugs. Monet watches the dandelion for the rest of the afternoon, because she wants to be there to see it get squashed. She is wondering: What is keeping the cars from zooming over it? How does it stay rooted with the vibrations from the delivery trucks?

IV

All week she's been trying to find a name for her lonely flower. The bud has opened up, there must be one hundred tiger-tooth-shaped petals showing. It is as tall as the curb. She is doing the dishes and she is pour- ing in the last bits of Dawn Liquid from the bottle and bubbles are flying in the air. She gets bubbles in her mouth and her nose. She is laughing at herself and as she laughs, she lets out a snort and the bubbles fly up. She is watching them come back down, and she likes the feel of them touch- ing her face. She thinks, "Bubbles! That is what I can name my flower."

V

That night Monet dreams for Bubbles. She can become a construc- tion worker wearing a red hard hat, building trellises for the other flowers and ladders for ants. Or an architect as rich as Dow Jones, with a pencil

I will Sing Life

behind her left petal. She imagines Bubbles working next to Mother Teresa in an orphanage for lost seeds, or with her own advice column: "Dear Bubbles, For the past three weeks my neighbor won't direct her roots to grow away from mine and I have, umpteen times, put in a complaint to the gardener but I haven't gotten any results. What shall I ever do? Signed, Beautiful and Overcrowded."

VI

The next morning, Monet washes out one of the pea cans from dinner and uses a can opener to cut out the bottom. Bubbles has been getting taller and she is worried about her. She gets a white sheet of paper, paints little flowers on it, and pastes it inside. She is still supposed to be resting indoors, but she sneaks out of the house when nobody's home. Up close, Bubbles is even more beautiful. Every little petal is like a hundred beams of not-too-hot sunshine. She knows it won't be lonely anymore because she's fooling it with the flowers and it can still take in the sun. The cars start to drive around her. They don't notice the flower but they notice the can, and who wants to feel their tires going over a can?

VII

Monet is back at the window listening to the drip from the drainpipe and the drops that fall into the pothole in the driveway. The road sounds different, instead of hissing it says, "shhhhh!" and the smell of wet dog is in the air from the strays. The kids that are down the street are screaming and cheering for each other to see how long it takes somebody to run off the porch on one side of the street and to the porch on the other side and to see how wet they get. "Go! Go! Run! Oooh, it only took him ten seconds!"

Herb walks out of the house wearing brown pants and a trench coat. Sophie is nagging him to wear galoshes but he has one foot in the car and he blows her a kiss before he closes the door. While he is backing up and turning the wheel, Monet's hands tighten on the windowsill. She knows he won't see the pea can. He backs up just enough that the wheel is touching the pea can and then he stops. But then he turns the wheel and knocks the can over.

Monet's hands are shaking, she is dressing, and she is having trouble because her hands are getting numb. "Maybe if I dress up really warm and the other kids do see me, they won't tell Ma that I went out when it's raining." She is sneaking, and she does not notice that she is outside the gate

and is still tiptoeing. She slides the pea can off and Bubbles is leaning to
the side where she should be straight and firm. Monet uses her hand like
a crutch to hold her up. She does not hear the kids hollering, and they do
not notice that she is crouching in the middle of the street with this little,
delicate flower in the middle of her hand. She sticks her tongue out and
tastes the saltiness of her tears and the rustiness of the rain sliding down
her face.

When she wipes her eyes, she notices pink slippers next to the pea
can. She knows they are old feet because they are wrinkly and she has
knee-high stockings rolled up to her knees. Sophie pulls an old teaspoon
out of the pocket of her housedress and hands it to Monet. "Come over to
my house, I'll get a pot, and we can plant her again."

Monet thinks she understands how the surgeons that she watched on
PBS feel. She thinks that she has sweat on her brows. "Can I get enough
root? Will she make it?"

Sophie takes her hand, trying to weave in and out of puddles, but
Monet, terrified for her flower, is not even picking up her feet when she
walks.

THREE cats jump off the furniture in the living room, scurrying to hide because there is a visitor. It is clean, but you see the dust. Some things that Sophie can reach have been dusted, whichever things they use often or near often. There is a little armchair with a stack of newspapers just as tall as it. They have a throw-over on the couch and an abundance of canned foods because they've lived through the depression and you never know, and the cans are dented from being there so long.

MONET sits at the table and puts her head in her hand. Her fingers are gripping her hair by the roots while the rain from her hair drips on her face. Sophie is in the closet looking for a pot and she is asking questions, trying to make her talk. "Well, how old are you?"

"Oh, I'm eleven. I'll be twelve in September."

"I never see you out playing with the rest of the kids."

"I stay in the house pretty much."

"I never see you leave to go to school with the rest of the kids."

"I'm on homebound. I have tutors that come and teach me."

"Why?"

"I have sickle cell. It makes me go in the hospital a lot."

Sophie gets the pot out of the closet and cleans it in the kitchen sink to get the dust out of it. "Okay, bring your little flower over."

Then Sophie puts her fist on her hip again, so she can think about which area in the house gets the best light.

"When I was a little girl I used to live in Italy and I remember we had a garden in the backyard and I was the youngest child. I had to do the weekly flower arrangements. I would sit in the garden to decide which flower looked better today, or which flower would look good in the sunlight that came into the hallway."

"Which flowers were your favorite?"

"I would say I loved forget-me-nots the most."

VIII

Ma brings a basin of water up to Monet's room and brushes her teeth, washes her face and her legs, puts socks and a clean pair of panties on her, and bundles her up to take her to the hospital. Monet lays in the back of the car, which Ma was warming while she was dressing her. Ma is asking, "Why did you go out there in the rain?"

With her head on the backseat, Monet is trying to push up so that she can get one last look at where Bubbles is staying, but she is too weak.

IX

"Bubbles? I just wanted to call and say hi, and ask what you've been up to and how are you doing after your accident? . . . I'm really calling to apologize about my not being around anymore to talk to you or to look at you. . . . I know, I know you miss me, I'm sorry that I got sick. It wasn't my fault. I tried to stay home, but Ma couldn't keep staying up with me so I had to come to the hospital. . . . No, not any longer than I have to. Sophie will change your water. Please wait for me."

She hears a velvety petaled sigh.

X

Monet is glad to be home again. She opens up the car door and slams it. "Ma, I'm gonna go say hi to Sophie for a second." She's hurrying, taking not-full steps from the stiffness. Sophie is sweeping.

"Hello, Monet, how are you? I talked to your sister Lilia and she told me that you've been in the hospital. Are you okay now?"

She cannot stand still for the conversation. Sophie is talking, but Monet stops her. "Can I go get Bubbles?" Sophie nods, giving her a soft-dentured smile. Monet opens the front door, not mindful to wipe her feet because she is too eager to find Bubbles.

She goes in to the living room and there is no green stem or yellow the color of the sun anywhere in the room. A sad brown stem holds a spikey gray ball. Over and over in her head she says, "This is not Bubbles, this is her pot but this is not Bubbles." She is gently stroking Bubbles's stem with the side of her thumb and she puts her head down and cries softly and just strokes her stem.

XI

She jumps because the front door that she should not have left open slams from the wind blowing through the kitchen. The breeze comes into the living room and wrenches Bubbles to the side. Her tired gray head hangs. Monet looks at Bubbles and she starts shaking her head.

Monet decides that she would rather have her own warm breath give Bubbles flight instead of some unknown breeze that is here for the moment and gone the next. Her hand trembles for a few seconds and then snaps the stem. She feels the juices of Bubbles on her fingers, the wet silky feeling, and she brings her outside. She closes her eyes for a second and takes in a breath, because she knows that when she exhales this air, she is letting go of all the beauty. She feels every motion of the air going

I Will Sing Life

up out of her lungs. As she blows, seeds lift off in a stream. The one hundred petals that used to be the color of not-too-hot sunshine are now fully in the stream of sunlight. They are dancing in a soft glide.

One seed lands in a crevice of a tree trunk, one floats over where a man is collecting bottles and it sticks in his hair. One drifts across Sophie's lawn past the other dandelions that won't turn gray till the end of the summer. But Monet follows the one that goes up high in the air, dancing weightlessly, bouncing off breezes from different directions. Sophie has been standing back and watching it all. She sees the stem that Monet has dropped, and she sweeps Bubbles back into her crack in the road. There is one little seed still holding on.

Corey Svien

FROM THE TIME he was seven, Corey has been drawing a family of teddy bears. One bear represents Corey, and he draws a bear for each of his friends who have helped him fight cancer. Like all teddy bears, they do not feel pain or fear, they always smile and have hope, and they never really die. If a teddy bear is missing some fur or some stuffing, that only means that it has been clasped tightly through many battles against the dark. Corey's three strongest bears are friends who lost hair, organs, and ultimately their lives to cancer. Corey, who rarely has hair and whose chest scar scored a perfect ten in a camp competition, is the next strongest.

Corey has been fighting cancer for twelve of his fourteen years, but his drawings of the teddy bears never show these scars. Since Corey has so often survived his own disease when it appeared that he would not, he no longer cares about appearances. When he draws his bears, he draws what he sees inside each of his friends.

Though Corey gathers strength from his imaginary teddy bears, he insists on their connection to real people fighting real problems. He does not use them to escape, but rather to welcome others into the world of fighting cancer. The teddy bears' arms are permanently open.

Those arms are open even to people much older than Corey. His friend Dottie recalls, "It was the most beautiful conversation I ever heard. My mother was afraid because she had cancer. Little Corey came over — he was thirteen years old and skinny as a matchstick, but he sat up so straight on the davenport explaining to her about life and death. She was eighty-six, just as thin as he was, and shrunk down to just his height. He told her he was not afraid of dying, that we are just here for a while and then we go to an even better place. My mother never talked about death to anyone, but she did with Corey. Then he got her talking about hope. He was so young and he had been through so much, but his faith was so strong. I thought of Jesus preaching to the elders. At the end, my mother said, 'For a little guy, you sure know a lot.' And you know, she got better, just like Corey."

This is just one of the many "Corey stories" his friends love to tell. Most of these friends are adults who thought Corey might need their help because, in addition to being sick, he has never met his father and chooses to live with his grandparents. These friends soon learned that it was often Corey who was helping them.

Corey is always at work on a new scheme for spreading his message. In a letter to Paul Newman, he suggested, "Maybe we can sneak you up to the hospital by putting you in surgeon's clothes — a gown, mask, booties, so no one will know it's you." On another occasion, he explained, "I don't think just having cancer is enough to get me on *Geraldo*. I guess I should commit a crime so it could be: 'Cancer Convicts, on the next *Geraldo*!' "

At home in Minnesota, Corey has become such a celebrity that he has received stuffed teddy bears from dozens of fans, including the governor. Since Corey likes to give, and since the room he shares with his brother is just big enough to fit their bunk beds, Corey often gives the bears away. We overheard one person to whom Corey gave a bear protest, "But, Corey, you love teddy bears," to which Corey replied, "I know, but I love you, too."

I DON'T draw a person as a Teddy Bear unless they are a Teddy Bear. I have to feel that their spirit is bright and caring. That's the only way. My Teddy Bears started in my imagination but they are linked with reality — they are symbols for real friendship, for real fighting together. They are great knights and fighters. They will defeat the most horrible things. For me and my friends, the thing the Teddy Bears are fighting against is cancer.

The Teddy Bears always fight by never giving up hope. Sometimes kids are afraid to fight a problem in reality — they don't want to be lying around suffering with a big scar on their side — but if they fight and win in their imaginations, they say, "Hey, I can do it!" and then they can win in reality, too. When there's a big crisis with your cancer, the bad stuff also happens in your imagination, and you have to fight it there, too. When you start using your imagination, you learn to fight not just with your mind but also with your soul, and if you do that you will win because the soul is the most powerful thing there is.

The imagination is even more powerful than a tumor. A tumor can only grow certain ways. It depends on the cancer and what stage you're in. But the imagination grows wonders. I don't know the limit of mine and I probably never will — it can't be limited. Imagination can go everywhere, it's a way of life and life can't end because there's something after life. But a tumor has limits — if it grows too big, it won't have nothing to grow on. If you look at the imagination and the tumor — one soars and the other gets stuck in the body.

For me, the Teddy Bears are symbols of fighting to get better. When I was around seven or eight, I was in for chemo and I was bored, so I started doodling. I liked teddy bears, so I started drawing them, then I started drawing characters like the Wiz Bear, but I wanted to do more than just draw characters, so I asked myself, "What do Teddy Bears really mean?" and I realized the answer was friendship. And the Wiz Bear that I had been drawing symbolized a friend who has courage. Then it came to me — a lot of things just come to me — that I should start drawing myself as Wiz Bear and my friends as Teddy Bears, too. I made Carrie into Carrie Bear, I made Pete into King Pete, I made my art therapist, Judith, into Meow.

The way I make a Teddy Bear is I think of a symbol of what a person likes or what they are like. Carrie likes owls, but she's more like a rabbit. She's cheerful, cuddly, she's got a lot of power, so her symbol is a rabbit. King Pete is like a king and he's always bright. Wiz Bear has the kind of sash they put medals on, but you can't see the medals because they are within. You don't need medals if you show off your spirit.

Sometimes Wiz Bear has a thunderbolt, because a thunderbolt is both light and power together, like hope and friendship. Like, if I'm in a big crisis, I draw the thunderbolt to remind me that friendship is near and that Carrie and Pete are fighting with me. I draw the thunderbolt when I need extra power but also when I feel I have extra power.

I don't think of my Teddy Bears as stuffed animals, I think of them as friends. Once or twice I've had to explain to people, "Listen, if you think my Teddy Bears are lame, you're thinking wrong. I don't play with stuffed animals." My Teddy Bears are connected to stuffed animals because when you are little, a stuffed animal takes away the bogeyman, and my Teddy Bears take away the cancer and the pain. The difference is that little kids put their friends into their teddy bears. If a little kid knew Carrie and Pete, he might put Carrie's smiling and caring, and Pete's ability to hope and survive and Anna's cheerfulness together in his teddy bear. He'd become imaginary friends with it because it's a symbol of those friends. But the Teddy Bears I use now are my *real* friends and then I draw them as teddy bears. I pick up the memory of stuffed animals because you have to re-member friendship in all the ways that you can. It makes a smile on your face when you have someone to protect you.

When I was first diagnosed, I was so scared that I didn't sleep for about six days. The doctors didn't know what to do. My grandma knew — she snuck my old teddy bear past the nurses even though it wasn't sterile, and I went right to sleep that night. I think a lot of adults still have a stuffed animal that they remember and still have adventures with, but they don't like to tell people about it; it's probably a secret matter.

When I was around two and a half, my kidney had a five-pound tumor. It was so big it closed my belly button. They had to do surgery to take it out. They put 286 stitches in me and I had lots of chemotherapy and radiation. All those strong drugs when I was that young wiped out my growth process and crippled me for a couple of months. I remember being totally stiff. They noticed I had finally started to move again when they saw I had pulled a tube out of my nose with my feet. I had learned to talk before I got sick, but when I couldn't move, I stopped talking. I had to learn to talk all over again.

I remember that it was a green room they had me in. It was scary. It looked like spinach. They're supposed to put pink and blue and all sorts of pretty stuff in a children's ward, not scary, ugly green. Get with it! It's in the old wing of the hospital. If you tried to find it you'd get lost, but I wouldn't. I never get lost in this joint.

When I started moving around in a wheelchair, I started racing and taking off. One time when I was only three, they left the station door open — bad mistake! I took off from the station and went AWOL. It was an awful place, and I just wanted to get out. I took the elevator down to the ground floor and was on my way to the front door when they found me. I freaked them out! They started locking the wheelchairs, but I started opening them. One time I almost hit a heart monitor that was in the hall, but I swooved and missed it. They started keeping me in a room where they could always see me.

I got out of the hospital after six months. When I was four, I went to preschool and they found out that I have a high-frequency hearing loss that almost deafened me so I was pretty much reading lips. I had learned to do it by watching the TV. I'm rusty, but I can still read lips well enough to watch TV in my room with the sound off when I'm supposed to be sleeping. I'm still kind of slow with speaking: some words I can't say, and sometimes I have a mental block that keeps me from remembering things.

After the surgery and all the chemo and radiation I got when I was two and three, I was cancer-clear for four years. If you make it to five years, they say you're cured. But it recurred in my lung when I was seven. I was a little bit scared, but I just realized: "Wait a minute, it's just a surgery and the doctors know what they're doing, I guess." The kind of cancer I have is called Wilms' tumor, and if it spreads it usually goes to the lungs. They went in and took out the tumor but they didn't get enough of it, so they gave me chemo again. They kept on doing this chemo and surgery, chemo and surgery, plus a whole bunch of tubes, portacaths, hickmans, lots of radiation. I had a bone marrow transplant in 1988, which worked for a while, but then my cancer came back to my right lung again, so I had some more chemo and another surgery and stuff. Each time I would get cancer-clear for a while, but then it would come back again to

I Will Sing Life

my right side. I've had surgeries for my teeth, my kidney, my lymph nodes, my lung a few times. I think I've had seventeen surgeries. It's probably written down somewhere in my files. I've seen all my files. There're twenty-two volumes — Encyclopedia Corey. But it's nothing to be happy about. I had to sit with my legs bent on my bed when they were wheeling me to surgery because there wasn't enough room on the tray for them to put all the files.

Usually kids don't have cancer for this long. I'm a rare case of Wilms' tumor. Normally, chemo and surgery works the first time or maybe the cancer recurs once. One kid in Minneapolis who had it when he was two just graduated from high school and he never had it again after they took out his kidney. I didn't want to have cancer for twelve years. You just don't know what's going to happen. I just live each day as it happens.

I'm not really scared when my cancer comes back and I need more surgery. I've been through it so many times, and I recovered before, so I might as well not be scared. But sometimes I'm just sick of it. I get sick of the tubes and everything else. I've had it so many times. They always cut along the same old scar from when I was two. It's so deep now it's pitiful. But I have to keep fighting it.

Last week they finally took the whole right lung out — the tumor was as big as a silver dollar and it was taking forty percent of my blood. The lung needed that much blood to live because it was really wrecked. It had been messed with too much by the surgeries, the tumor, and the chemo. The tumor takes a lot of your food, too. The lung would have probably died anyway, or I would have. It needed all the energy that I need.

Now that they've taken it out, I feel warmer. There's more blood getting to my toes. And now I'm cancer-clear again and I think there's a wonderful chance of being cured. There're no more organs left in me for the cancer to go to.

The other thing I have — it's not related to the cancer — is Wolff-Parkinson-White syndrome. It's an extra muscle in my heart that forms a canal that heartbeats can go through, so I have extra heartbeats. The extra heartbeats are not really smart and they go the wrong way and then I can feel my heart go faster and faster and faster, up to two hundred beats per minute. When I take medicine, it's supposed to slow down, but it hasn't been working. A few weeks ago, they tried a test to find the medicine that would slow down my heart, but it made my heart go slower and slower until it stopped for a couple of seconds and they had to start it up again. It was weird going that close, but not going *too* close. People say, "I saw a

light but then I came back into my body," but I didn't see anything, so I wasn't that close. I woke up with someone putting air in me with one of those pumps.

A lot of people think that your heart is you. It's not really your heart, it's your soul. The heart is just a symbol of the soul because it beats all the time and it's precious to your body. A soul is the person inside. It's what's important to each person. You can't just draw it. The symbol I make for each Teddy Bear is a symbol of its soul.

WHEN people hear all the stuff I've been through they say, "Whoa, how can you live your whole life like that?" I tell them I'm down here for some goal. No one knows their goal until they've achieved it. Even death could be a goal God wants you to achieve. I'm not done with my goal yet, which is to help people. I think the reason a lot of people have cancer is so that they can help others and learn about life. I learned how to cope with cancer. I know the routes and I know the angles. I've been through the pain, so I can tell other people what's gonna happen. They might be scared —

I Will Sing Life

yeah, you have to be scared sooner or later — but they'll learn it's gonna happen and then it's gonna be over. I can tell them that I was scared, too, but if you think about it for a while there's nothing to be scared of. You have people and hope to help you. The thing you're gonna be scared of is dying, but you don't have to be scared, because dying is not the end.

From living my whole life with cancer I've learned to always fight a problem: I was deaf and I learned to read lips; I couldn't move and then I went AWOL; I wasn't supposed to live past age five and here I am. If they say I can't drive a car because all the medicine has made me too short, then I'll just sit on a phone book. I like to get better.

The Teddy Bears are a really important part of fighting the problems of cancer. It's not the drugs and stuff that's the worst problem with cancer; it's friends dying and suffering. I have more friends from the hospital than from school. I've lost five friends. The leaders of the Teddy Bears are Wiz Bear, Carrie Bear, and King Pete. Carrie and Pete have both died, but they're still living as Teddy Bears. The Teddy Bears are a way to bring my friends back to life.

I think there's no one who is more of a Teddy Bear than Carrie. Before I met her I had heard that when she was thirteen she had lost her leg, but she didn't give up. It was only a leg; it didn't matter to her. I said to myself, "Whoa, she didn't even complain about that? That's the way I have to deal with it." When I met her, she was eighteen and had had cancer for five years. I saw how she always had a smile on her face and she always cared. A lot of people said we were part of each other's adopted family. I was like her little brother. There were times when I helped her and other times when she helped me. Once, I didn't want to have lung surgery, and she said, "You've got to have it done. You've had them before, you can have them again." Carrie Bear is one of the strongest bears I've made. Her soul is so mighty that even when she's in the deepest pain she wants to help others.

Carrie was twenty-two years old and she had a cheerful, weird kind of death. No one knew it was coming, but she fought on even with all of the suffering she had. She was unconscious for a while and she was pretty much at the end of dying, but when I came to visit her, she woke up. They said she'd been out of it for hours. There were about fifteen people waiting, and I came in. I said, "Hi, Carrie, keep on fighting." And she opened her eyes, took my hand, asked me to sit near her, and said, "I love you, Corey," and then mumbled and stuff. Even with the deepest pain she had a smile. Now I know that she's not suffering anymore.

Carrie fought cancer for nine years. At her funeral I talked about death and Carrie. I told them death is just the next stage in life and you should just be happy because she's not suffering anymore. It still makes me feel better to talk to her. I know she's listening. I feel that she's around when I need her.

PETE'S symbol used to be a moon, because the moon was a light in the darkness. Anywhere he goes there's a light and his soul is bright. I talked to him sometimes, but not much. I wanted to spend more time with him. We met in a support group. He came and visited me when I was in for the bone marrow. He died a few weeks after he visited me. He was thirteen and I was eleven. He had just got out of a bone marrow, too. I saw him and I said, "He did it, so I have to do it." I saw lots of courage in his eyes and his smile and how he acted and everything else in him. He died while I was in for the bone marrow, but no one told me until later. When I found out, I thought, "He's more than a moon, he's a king because he's so loyal and brave, he should become a king," so I made him into King Pete. I'm kind of a leader of the Teddy Bears, and he's a king that takes care of the people.

ANNA was my age but went to a different school. She was cheerful and she liked to draw rainbows and butterflies — she adored butterflies. She had a brain-stem tumor on one side of her brain. She lost control of her arm, her leg, and her eyesight on one side. When her body was going, she suddenly drew half a butterfly. That was all she could see, or maybe she thought that since half of her body was gone there was no point in draw-

I will Sing Life

ing it. She was eleven when she died. They said she was going to live for six months at the most, and she lived eighteen months. We met at support group and wrote each other notes and interviewed each other. For the first few weeks that she knew me she always giggled and she didn't stand next to me at the support group because she was so shy about holding my hand. Anna Bear's symbol is a rainbow. Sometimes I draw her with a butterfly body and a Teddy Bear head.

TEDDY Bears aren't afraid of dying. Your body is a thing but your soul is not. Your body is just like a home — you're renting this condo for a few years and then you have to move somewhere else. If you think of your body as you, you'll go: "Aaaah! I've got cancer! This is the end!" But if you think of it my way, you'll think: "Yeah, okay, I've just got to live with it. My body is just the place I'm living right now until I go to a new place." If someone created a masterpiece, they're not going to throw it away after seventy-five years. That's something your soul is, a masterpiece.

I know Heaven is gonna be the best. Just wait and see. It's so good you can't imagine it. It's like each person's own land of imagination. And your imagination usually isn't scary, because it's you. I think of Heaven as a big old space where friends come together. It won't be like the descriptions of Heaven that are so lameoid — harps and stuff. Get with it. I bet God does it good. He's more than a Teddy Bear. He's the spirit behind the Teddy Bears. He probably makes it modern each year, because there are all those inventors who have died.

But just because Heaven is great doesn't mean you can think, "Oh, big deal. I have to die some time or other." You don't want it to happen. You want to be around with your friends. If you're scared, that's all right. Everyone is scared, but remember, if you have friends who care, then you'll want to get better to be with them.

I've got lots of friends who have helped me fight. My friends are one of the good things that have come out of cancer for me. I don't know how I met them all. I have friends who know me that I don't even know. I have so many friends in the hospital, all the doctors and nurses. I've made like a family from all the adults I'm friends with. I've never met my real dad, and my mom has some problems that she should be fighting, so I live with my grandma and grandpa. When there's problems at home, sometimes I'd rather be in the hospital. If you've been to a certain station a lot of times, get to know the nurses, it'll be fun. When they don't have to do stuff, they'll stop by to say hi. They might even give you a birthday party.

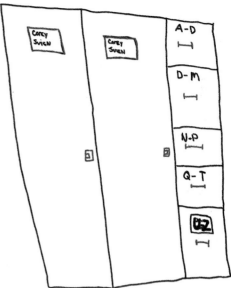

Dr. Krivit at his Office

You can take the speakers out of their phones if you want to play a practical joke on them.

ONCE Judith, Carrie, Carrie's sister, and I were at the hospital and we wanted to go to the We-Can Weekend for families of people with cancer, but since none of us had family that was coming with us, we filled out the application saying we were "The Teddy Bear Family." We were like a family to each other.

At first it was hard to make Dr. Krivit into a Teddy Bear because Teddy Bears are supposed to make you feel good, and lots of kids hate their doctor. Dr. Krivit is the doctor in charge of me. He's a get-down-to-business guy. If we go into the room, he'll say, "Well, here it is . . . ," and be open about everything because he knows I want to know. The doctors think I'm crazy, but I like to watch the shots go in. It doesn't make it hurt more for me, because I've been around for a while. Some other doctors don't tell me what's happening and I say, "Tell me *now!* Or I'm not gonna let you do it."

Barb George was supposed to just be a volunteer who stopped by and said hi while I was in the bone marrow transplant unit. Usually you're supposed to visit and then go on to another person, but it didn't really work that way because her spirit and mine, we didn't quit. I would go to her apartment a lot and watch movies. If I need to get out of the house, she'll get me out of the house. I named Barb "Smiley Bear." She arranged for me to go to the Hole in the Wall Gang Camp. Now she has a baby named Alissa and I draw her as "Cutie Bear."

Jackie, she's like a baker. I started helping teach at the Sunday school and we became friends and I went over to her house. We like to cook together and talk a lot about cancer. Her husband, Rick, he's going to school to become a minister because he likes reading the Bible a lot. He's a neat guy to talk to.

A LOT of people are trying to fatten me up. It's crazy. I'll fatten up when I want. My friend Tom's not helping a bit. He comes up to my hospital room and eats all my food. I tell him to bring me food and he eats half of it. One time Tom made a bet with me that if I could eat a Whopper with cheese (740 calories), he would kiss the floor. He had to get down there, with all those people around looking at him, and he kissed the floor for five minutes! He's a joker, but he has a serious manner part of the time, and when you see him talking to the "I Can Cope" support group you say, "Whoa!" because of all the ways he cared about his family when he was going through cancer.

Judith, my art therapist, she has the creativity. When I'm with her, I come up with ideas out of nowhere. She is more like a cat with her creativity. She's quiet when she draws. Her masks and her drawings all turn out looking like she made them. You can tell she's a cat because she's quiet and mysterious. Cats are like that: they sneak around because they want to know what's happening. Judith is always curious about what artwork I'm doing. She always wants to keep it when I want to throw it out.

Mary Hastings brings me "room service" from The Big Ten Subshop whenever I'm in the hospital. She always has a smile and some Mountain Dew when she comes. She has a good sense of humor. She has lots of connections and she can feel if something is happening. She somehow knew that my heart was beating faster once, and she called the Emergency Room and I was there. I think she has an instinct for that. She likes doing her work, which is helping the hospital with special programs. She's the big boss on the Land of Imagination project that I helped to start.

MY grandma and grandpa are very nice. They work hard but take time to stay home a lot for my brother, Jason, and me and my cousins when they come over for the weekend. Jason and I are always bugging each other, but we really do care about each other.

I RELATE better to adults and to other kids with cancer. Other children don't know how to deal with their feelings about cancer because they're kept away from all the info. They haven't lived close to death and suffering, so they don't feel the information of life. They'll see a kid like me and they'll be scared. Some kids want to be as nice as possible so they won't hurt me. Some kids just leave and don't want to come around. It happens because they're scared.

One kid — I normally just forget about things like this, but I needed to teach one kid a lesson. He was laughing because I was bald, so I said to myself, "Well, why not this once? Just to do it for the heck of it," so I said to him, "Hey! You don't know what you're talking about, do you? I have cancer and I have to have chemotherapy and I lost my hair because of that, so why don't you shut up and eat your lunch!" I didn't mean to be

mean, I did it just that once, because the other kids were doing it, too. Then he ends up writing me a note later on, saying he was sorry.

A lot of kids and adults with cancer are embarrassed — they want to wear wigs because they've lost their hair — but I think just forget about it and have fun with it. If I'm bald, I write stuff on my head. Once I wrote, "Touch this and die!"

I just want to be treated normal. My friend Tom, he says he treats me normal and I say, "Heck, no, you treat me worse." He couldn't say anything back because he gave up making fun of me for Lent.

THE Hole in the Wall Gang Camp is one place where everyone knows about cancer. All the kids there have learned to live through things. We know we're normal people and we want to fight our problems together. We just want to be together and have freedom — no doctors going after us. There's a lot of the Teddy Bear feeling at camp. You see all the smiles, you feel so much energy.

Writing and singing a song called "The Teddy Bear Feeling" was my favorite thing at camp. The first year I did it as a folk song, but then this year we did it as a doo-wop rock-and-roll song. We got all the counselors singing backup, and the kitchen crew made T-shirts. My counselor, Gary, played the synthesizer, and we made up dance steps. It was a really big thing. Next summer we're gonna do it as a rap. The chorus goes:

I got the Teddy Bear Feeling
We fight with Love in our hearts.
We are going to fight together.
I got the Teddy Bear Feeling.
I got the Teddy Bear Feeling.

I went fishing with Paul Newman this summer. He rowed us to his favorite secret fishing spot, which will still remain secret. He put my bait on and said, "Here's Superworm!" But then my hook came back without Superworm and I said, "The death of Superworm!" and sang taps. Then he said, "Here's Superduperworm," but I still didn't catch nothing. He put his life jacket on funny. He put it on, but then he didn't put one arm in. He's good. He's a fun guy. I don't think he likes being around crowds; he likes to get away and go fishing. I made a Teddy Bear that is Paul Newman, he's called Gold Nugget Bear, but I've been keeping it a secret since Paul Newman is kind of private. He's got blue eyes but I drew sunglasses over them so no one would recognize him.

ON the last night of camp we put a candle in the middle of the room and talked about our favorite things like going swimming, the dance, throwing whipped cream in Randy's face. You get so emotional, you don't want to leave, you can't leave, but you know you have to. A lot of people left crying and just remembering.

EVEN if I get cured of cancer, I will still have it mentally, because I will always be fighting it as a friend of people who have it. I'll be on the other side, but it'll still be like having cancer because when one person has cancer all his friends and family have it, and when I help others I'll remember mine. If anyone said that when they get cured they want to forget about having cancer, I'd say, "Shove it!" If you're cured of cancer and you stop fighting, then you're pretty much a loser because you're not helping others. And even if you never had cancer or no one in your family had cancer, you should help, too. There should be one volunteer for each person with cancer. That could happen.

That's why I want to be a child specialist, and help kids cope with their feelings, get their minds off it and make sure they have hope. That's one thing I have to get through their heads. They need to have hope from doing other things. Like the Teddy Bears, they give me power to live. It's not only you that's suffering. It's your whole family, your friends, everyone you know, everyone you will know. If you're not strong, they won't be strong, because you've lost hope.

Hope started in the world at the same time bad things started, because when there's negative, there's positive. Bad things like cancer aren't a punishment; they're a way of learning. It's a hard way of learning because of all the suffering, but it's probably the only way. If it wasn't for the bad things that happened to me, I wouldn't know so much about hope.

Corey Svien died a few months after this chapter was completed, before being photographed for this book. His cancer returned undetected and filled the space from which his lung had been removed. On July 3, after talking to a friend on the phone, Corey told his grandfather that he was having trouble breathing. A few seconds later he said, "Happy Fourth of July," and then collapsed. He remained unconscious but alive until Independence Day. Corey was buried with a teddy bear and a liter of Mountain Dew, in the grave next to Carrie's.

Shawn Valdez

SHAWN SIGNED UP for poetry writing because, in order not to hurt any of the activity directors' feelings, he decided to go to each camp activity once. Having just turned seven, he did not really know what poems were, so he had no reservations about writing them. His mode of composition was that of a wandering nature poet with a secretary; he would walk up to a plant, a stump, a leaf, and talk to it. We walked behind him and took dictation.

His poems were about life and death. Shawn had come to camp with a few weeks left to live. His leukemia had relapsed a second time, and his doctor and family had decided to take him off chemotherapy. His only medication was prednisone, a steroid to give him a bit more energy and reduce pain. Shawn had not been told his prognosis; everyone wondered how much he knew.

Shawn fell in love with Tadger, a mystical animal too shy to leave his home in the woods by day. Tadger has a mailbox at the Hole in the Wall Gang Camp in which campers drop letters. When everyone is asleep, Tadger delivers his replies to these letters, and leaves treats and glittery paw prints in the cabins. Shawn wrote to Tadger every rest period, enclosing presents he had made in arts and crafts.

A few days into camp, Shawn started telling people, "I don't have leukemia anymore." We did not know if this meant that he was too happy to feel sick, or that he had confused the end of his chemotherapy with the end of his cancer.

Shawn went home at the end of his session and the camp staff waited in dread for news about him. When the news finally came, it was that Shawn had been miraculously correct. Word raced around camp: "Shawn does not have leukemia anymore!" He had experienced a complete spontaneous remission. The doctors did not understand it — nobody with such advanced T-cell leukemia had ever gone into remission taking only a steroid. Finally, they asked Shawn for his own explanation. He replied, "Tadger cured me."

WHEN Tadger learned that he and Shawn were going to be in a book, he sent us a few of the letters that Shawn had written to him during the summer, noting that they were only the surface of a much deeper friendship. In Tadger, Shawn had found a friend who understood what it is like to be small, shy, and wary of the grown-ups' doubts, but still young, untamed, and able to live on love and fun alone. They both suspect that maybe the rules of medical science apply only when you believe in them.

Shawn's doctors do not know what cured him, and they are uncertain of how to prevent another relapse, a relapse that would again leave him with few medical options. Shawn does not want to think about these uncertainties. Six months after camp, he has time only for the "love and fun," which he says made him better, and to perfect his Nintendo playing, which he says helps him to forget. The winter of doctors, needles, and fear is behind him; he will not discuss it. Now, even the poems he writes about cancer are full of joy and forgetting.

Shawn's family and friends, who have found it harder to forget, were the ones who told us most of his story. Since Shawn believes that love made him well, the voices of the people who love him are at the heart of the story of his illness, his miraculous recovery, and his uncertain present.

This chapter is constructed out of Shawn's poems and letters, and out of direct quotations from interviews with Shawn, his family, and friends. Paula Hinson, Shawn's attitudinal healing counselor, told us about an occasion that we have tried to recreate: "It was his family, a lot of friends, like a big support group. Everybody wanted to know how Shawn got better. They'd heard he'd been in a hospice program and everybody was sitting around the table, talking about what chemo protocol it was and what Dr. Pitel had to say and what this doctor had to say and what-do-you-think-could-have-happened, and nobody could explain it. Just analyzing it to pieces, until Shawn looked up, and sighed, and rolled his eyes, put his head on his elbows, and said, 'Don't you understand, it's just a *miwacle?*' "

Cast of Characters

MARIA: *My Mom. Nobody is better than my Mommy.*

What if you didn't have your Mom?
Nobody to rock you to sleep?
Nobody to feed you?
Nobody to care about you?
Nobody to share feelings?

IVONNE: *My sister, she's seventeen. She's really a teenager. She's grumpy in the morning and she sleeps in when she's supposed to go to work. She's beautiful, she's cool, and she's awesome, and she took me to the library when I've never been to the library.*

J.P.: *He's my big brother, he's nine. He's a bully. Cain and Abel is my favorite Bible story but not because I would ever really kill J.P. Sometimes he calls me names and calls me crybaby and then I say stuff about him that I don't really mean — like idiot, idiotic, brainless.*

LEE: *My stepbrother, he's ten. He came to live with us last year. If I hadn't met Lee I wouldn't know about Nintendo because he's the first person who showed us how to play Nintendo. He shares a room with me and J.P. and it gets pretty messy in there.*

TERRY: *My stepdad. I call him Dad, though. He's kind, I love him, he lets me do stuff, but not as much as my mom. When I have spinal taps, he holds my hand and tells me to breathe deeply.*

I Will Sing Life

DR. PITEL: *My doctor. He's funny, he chases me around.*

PAULA: *She works at Aslan House. She helps me to think about Nintendo and relax when I get chemo. She made tapes that helped me relax. I used to listen to them every night.*

MISS O'SULLIVAN: *We call her Miss O. She's my second-grade teacher. She's nice to me. She lets me sleep in the rocking chair when I get real tired.*

JANET: *She sits behind me at school. She's my friend and I like her, but she always wants to take care of me and I already have a mother.*

SHAWN: God doesn't choose you to be sick. You just go outside and catch something or eat off the floor, or it's cold. But He helps when you do get sick.

The only thing I remember is when I was diagnosed. First I had a high fever at my house in December three years ago. Then I fell asleep. When I woke up I was in the car. And my dad, Terry, and my mom were driving me and I was wondering what was happening. So I asked my dad, "Where are we going?" and he said, "To the hospital." I said, "Why?" and he said, " 'Cause you're sick." I fell asleep in the car and then I woke up in the hospital. They did tests. I remember nobody telling me I had leukemia. I don't remember anything else from then. All I ever remember is fun things.

When I started treatment, it was kind of scary, especially with the chemo. I had to get stuck with needles. The first time it made me scared. When I got chemo, I started to lose my hair. Every time I lay down on the pillow there was hair on it. I was surprised and I was kind of a little worried. Mostly when I started to get bald I'd wear lots of hats, but that made it itchy 'cause it was falling out, so my mom was always washing my hat. It doesn't really matter if your hair is falling off. When I'm bald, everybody likes me better. I don't know why.

MARIA: He was first diagnosed when he was five. Then we started a chemotherapy protocol and he went in remission and everything was going fine until the end of August, two years ago. Shawn was supposed to go into first grade and we went for a checkup. They took blood, and his platelets were almost gone. He had relapsed

in his bone marrow. He was feeling okay, though. There was nothing terrible. That was when Dr. Pitel reevaluated everything, and the possibility of a bone marrow transplant in Gainesville came up, and he put Shawn on the waiting list for a bed in the transplant unit. From August until December when we finally got a bed, he was in a very intense protocol. We had to spend three days in the hospital every other week and he would get chemo around the clock. He went back in remission pretty quickly, but Dr. Pitel said the trick was to keep him in remission until the transplant, because if he relapsed again the chances were less and less.

J.P.: When they needed someone for the bone marrow transplant they tested mine. They gave me a shot and they took blood. I was kind of hoping it would match because I wanted to help Shawn, but also hoping it wouldn't because I knew it would kind of hurt. And I didn't want to give him my bone marrows if I had to stay in the hospital all the time.

MARIA: All of us were tested for matches for the transplant. A few days later, Shawn's nurse called. I could hear all the nurses in the background just dancing; the tests said Ivonne was a perfect match for him. So it was like Shawn was going to be born again. A new chance. We were going to forget about leukemia, get rid of that thing forever. I asked Ivonne again. I said, "You are a match; do you want to go ahead and do it?" and she said, "Don't be silly, Mummy, of course I want to."

SHAWN: Ivonne was the donor. I'm glad I got it from her. Think what would have happened if I had it from my brother. I'd be so wild. She got pretty sick after it. That made me sad. We had separate rooms at the hospital. She was in the room beside me.

If Ivonne had given me a brain transplant, I'd be a teenager and
    spend more time on the phone.
If Ivonne had given me her feet, I'd wear more shoes.
If Ivonne had given me a heart transplant, I'd give more hugs to me.
If Ivonne had given me her hair, I'd cut it.
If Ivonne had given me her eyes, science would be harder.
And if Ivonne had given me her smile, I'd look like a rose blooming
    and I'd use it on girls.

IVONNE: There was no doubt in my mind that I would do it. Everyone was, like, "Oh, it's such a *good* thing you're doing." I never really saw it in that way. I'm just thinking: Your mother or your brother or anyone else is in that position, you do it. It was scary, but then at the same time, it was for him. I'd never been in a hospital overnight before, and the I.V. was awful. They stuck two huge big needles right into my hips — I still have scars — they tap it out slowly, and this white liquid comes out. I thought it was going to be something else. But it was cool, because the moment it was out, it was going into Shawnie. It's cool that my chromosomes are in him now. Me inside him. And there was something good about being kind of uncomfortable for a week or two afterward. Because Shawn was *so* uncomfortable for such a long time.

MARIA: It was scary, it was very scary because I knew that he might die. The second possibility was that it might not be successful — he could get that graft-versus-host disease. And the third was that it

would not get rid of the leukemia. But Dr. Pitel said that it was the way to go, having such a perfect match.

Just going to the transplant unit was pretty scary, because you see some of the little ones dying. When we got there a thirteen-year-old girl died and then another one, and I thought, "Gosh, I hope we make it out of here."

SHAWN: After my bone marrow transplant, I had to stay in an isolation room for one hundred days. One hundred days or ninety-nine, I can't remember. It was pretty boring. The room was only as big as two of my bed. I played Nintendo about five hours a day, and the rest of the time I played with the nurses, or talked on the phone to Matthew, who was in the isolation room next door. I couldn't go outside. The only time I ever saw snow in my life was when I was in there and I didn't get to play in it. They wouldn't let my mom stay overnight at that hospital. She had to wear a mask, and special foot things.

I Will Sing Life

Isolation Room

When I was in the isolation room, there were no china doll monkeys
    hanging off the I.V. poles kissing their socks.
There were no strawberry-orange giraffes peeking in the windows.
Definitely no pair of the doctor's black Ninja Turtle underwear
    showing on TV.
No righteous Oreos invading my mouth.
And no minky-kinky tennis shoes dancing the cha cha on my walls.
There were no glittery purple semi-trucks driving their tires in my
    red Jell-O going rrrrr. . . .
And there were no teachers on unicycles delivering my food tray to
    me on their heads.
When I was in the isolation room, there was only a big green sign
    saying DO NOT ENTER in gigantic, black, mean stupid letters.

J.P.: I couldn't go in there, even with an isolation suit. I saw him
    through the window. I missed him. I kept on calling him on the
    phone. I would wake him up and we would talk about Nintendo.

MARIA: He kept himself pretty well entertained in there. The teacher
    would come in with the computer; he loved that. And he had his
    Nintendo, that was the main thing, and he'd talk on the telephone
    to Matthew. The physical therapist would come so he could exer-
    cise. It was terrible because he was living in a little bedroom, day
    in and day out.

   Terry used to leave Gainesville at 4:30 every morning to have
    time to get to Jacksonville for work, and I'd stay in bed until I
    could go be with Shawn. One morning, very early, someone called
    me over the intercom and said, "Mrs. Valdez, you have a phone
    call." So I'm exhausted, exhausted. I get the telephone and I'm still
    asleep and this lady says to me with a French accent — I didn't
    know it was Paula until much later on — "This is Madame So-and-
    so. How are you doing this wonderful morning? I'm here to grant
    you a wish. What do you wish on this Christmas?" So here I am
    with tears in my eyes telling her that the only thing I want is for
    my baby boy to be fine. And she's keeping all cool — "Okay. Yes,
    that's fine, your second wish? . . ." And I'm thinking, "What can I
    add?" I'm really thinking that someone is granting me all these
    wishes!

I went back to bed and she called about thirty minutes later now with her regular voice, "Hi Maria, how are you? I just felt this need to call. Something told me I need to talk to you."

TERRY: Probably what she was doing was checking to see how Maria was *really* doing. You get sick of people saying, "Oh, poor thing." You want to say, "Get out of my face."

MARIA: I mean I was going crazy. I didn't want to talk to anybody. And once in a while for her to come up with something crazy like that, it gets your mind completely off the problem. It makes you realize, "Hey, wait a minute, there's something, some *life* beyond this."

PAULA: I really don't know where I get these ideas. They just strike me. I'm very tuned in to the kids, a special antenna or closeness. Sometimes I'll have dreams in which I'm told that I should call the children.

A lot of times I know Maria won't call me because she feels, "Oh, I'm calling her and asking too much," or "I don't want to bother her," so sometimes I need to lovingly trick people. They're just jokes, I'm a jokester, that's the truth of it. I love to hear people laugh; laughter is so healing.

MARIA: During the transplant we used Paula's "Creating Love, Hope, and Miracles" tapes constantly, day and night, especially when Shawnie was not feeling well. His counts were very, very low, he had no energy, no white cells, nothing. The nurses were trained to put the tapes on and he was able to relax. He'd wake up and say, "My tummy hurts," or "I feel like throwing up," and I would say, "Well, close your eyes and listen to your tapes." It was kind of like "Hold on to your teddy bear. You're going to feel okay."

These tapes and these sessions with Paula really helped because he seemed so much in control of himself. They helped all of us. The boys and Terry and I were all listening to them and learning to relax. And then listening to the tapes, it was amazing, because Shawn was able to relax and would go to sleep and you would count one two three and he was gone, *gone,* you could not wake him up. He was somewhere else.

I Will Sing Life

PAULA: The tapes were done for all the people I couldn't see myself, but Shawn and I worked together to create something that works especially for him. For instance, when he was first diagnosed and he had given up eating, he was always anxious and worried. Well, every time Shawn wanted to get himself to eat, instead of being nauseated, we taught him to use his magic Nintendo button. He would press his fingers together, and that helped him remember playing Nintendo, which was a happy memory, and that made him able to eat.

Maria brought Shawn to my house in his pajamas late one night because he was anxious about shots he was going to get the next day. We were lying by the fire and the cat came in and I said, "Shawnie, wouldn't it be really neat if tomorrow you were really relaxed just like you're here with me in front of the fireplace, just like you love the kitty's soft fur being on you? Feel his paw, feel his fingernails . . . it's just a little scratch, and the kitty's doing that because it loves you. When you get stuck tomorrow, you're gonna feel just as comfortable and loved and just as relaxed as you feel right in my house." He didn't cry when they stuck him the next day.

MARIA: One day I called Paula because Shawn was having trouble getting back into chemo, especially the shots. The volunteer at Aslan House said she wasn't there. I said I wanted to have Paula talk to him before he had the shots. And the guy says, "Shawn Valdez? Just tell Shawn to leave his body. He's done it before." I said, "What? Why don't *you* tell him that?" And he did, and I heard Shawn saying, "Okay . . . All right, okay . . . Bye." I said, "Shawn, do you know how to leave your body?" He said, "Yup," but he didn't want to tell me how.

TERRY: For a few weeks after that, it was the joke at home: "What? You don't like that broccoli? Well, just leave your body. Ask Shawn how to do it."

PAULA: The positive imagery and relaxation techniques are ways of learning that you're more than just your body. When you focus on something else, you tend to forget about the physical and emotional pain. He knows how to do that very, very well. With him it's

more like "I'm in a fun place, playing Nintendo." He just forgets about his body and leaves that alone.

J.P.: After he came home from being in the isolation room, he couldn't touch the rugs because they were dusty, he couldn't touch anything, and he had to wear a mask. We had to clean whatever he was about to touch with Clorox. There was a big cleanup before he came home. The only thing we didn't have to clean was the Nintendo, because it had been with him in the hospital.

MARIA: A few weeks after the transplant, we felt so positive. We were looking forward to a normal life and I took him to the clinic to have his catheter removed because he wasn't supposed to need any more chemo. I was waiting for the bloodwork to come back and I saw the nurse come in with a little piece of paper. I looked at her face, and my heart just fell. I pulled the paper out of her hand, saw the counts, and went running into Dr. Pitel's office; he had not seen it yet, and I said, "Look," and he was just in shock. He said, "Oh, Jesus."

DR. PITEL: He was incurable. We discussed trying to put him back in remission, undergoing a second transplant, but the chances of being cured were just about zero. It was an extreme long shot, and most transplant centers in the United States weren't going to touch him. So eventually we elected to do nothing. Just give him pain medication and give him transfusions as he needed them.

TERRY: It was a shock, because everything was going so well — you have to absorb that kind of news for a few minutes. At first you think, "Okay, we'll just have to do something different." But Pitel was actually saying that nothing could be done. Period.

MARIA: Suddenly Dr. Pitel was saying, "I cannot take care of him anymore. I cannot do anything. Call hospice." That's not the way he said it, but I understood that he had to say, "You need help that I'm not able to give you." That was the only time I'd ever seen him cry.

He didn't want to tell me, but I kept on asking, "You know by experience; you treat these children with leukemia. How long? Tell me how long do I have left with him?"

Finally he said, "Maria, if he keeps getting platelets every day, the way he's going he'll be gone in three or four weeks. Whatever you want to do with him, do it now. Don't wait." So I went ahead and planned his birthday ahead of time. He always wanted to have a huge birthday party, so we had his whole class. Then, after that — this was for me — I wanted him to make his first Communion. Usually children do it when they are eight years old. I wanted him to because I had a very wonderful religious experience doing my first Communion at that age. Being so little, I really closed my eyes and Jesus was with me and I was playing with Him. That was giving something to my son whom I might not have for too long.

Before the first Communion it was not only Pitel telling me, I saw it with my own eyes. His little face, his color, his energy was gone. I just knew he wasn't going to last very long. There was no hope.

IVONNE: I had been doing some really stupid stuff. I had never really dealt with the feelings I had. I went out and went out and went out. After the transplant, I slowly eased back into church and praying. Then he relapsed again, and I just let go of everything. I didn't care about school; my grades dropped. There were times when I just couldn't deal with people. Everything just seemed so trivial and silly and foolish. I got a lot of easy grades then that I didn't deserve. That used to bug me so bad. I felt like: "If I deserve a D, give me a D. My little brother may be dying, but hey, I want a D! I want a damn D!"

DR. PITEL: He was developing a rash, so based on some experience I've had in the past, I said, "Well, let's just put him on a little bit of prednisone. Maybe it'll kill a few leukemia cells, and he'll feel better for a little while. After a few days he was feeling better, so I said, "All right, we'll keep him on the prednisone; he'll keep using it until it stops working."

MARIA: Paula called me and said, "You're going to let Shawn go to camp, aren't you?" and I said, "Are you *kidding?* What camp?" But she kept on asking me, "Is he going to go to camp?" and I said, "Paula, I don't think so. He's getting platelets every other day."

PAULA: It's funny, it was Shawn that was pushing me about camp and I didn't know what to tell him. I said, "It's up to your mom," and he said, "Well, call her and ask her," so I called her and said, "Maria, have you made any decisions about what you want to do?"

MARIA: I had mixed feelings about it. First of all, he wanted to go and then I heard about the camp and knew he would have a wonderful time. With Mummy and Daddy around, sometimes it is not good, because we are worried — Mummy with tear-eyes and Shawn saying, "Get me out of here." . . . He can always look at me and sense my worries.

When I first asked Dr. Pitel about going to camp, he said, "Well, let's wait and see how he does next week, let's wait and see how he does in these next few days."

Last year, when he went to a camp nearby, it was not as hard as this time, but it was hard. He was just five years old and had never been away, but I knew he was going to be fine. Then it was

"I'm going to miss my baby." This time it was serious. It was more "Let's see how it's going to feel not having him around." Him being in a safe place, but far away. Do you understand what I'm saying? I had some of that feeling inside, that curiosity. It was like a practice.

At the same time I was feeling that he'd be fine, he'd be having fun, being loved, and experiencing a lot of things that he hadn't experienced before. And he really wanted to go. There was no doubt. He was so excited. There was not one moment when he had any doubts. He was *going*. You should have seen him packing that little suitcase. Over and over and over again. Making sure he had everything he needed. I started having hope. I started realizing maybe there was something very good going on.

TERRY: Some of the things I had to say to Maria then I never really wanted to say. By the time he went to camp he was not supposed to have been here, period, but I thought it was a good idea to let him go and let him experience life himself. Maria, too, needed to let go and deal with these things for herself. For the past year and a half everything had been focused on him. She had to learn to let go — she seemed to be getting more and more caught up in it. She was assuming more responsibility than she should: "Could I have done something else? Maybe if I had done this instead of that?" That kind of thinking just didn't make sense, because everyone had done everything possible. I guess a lot of things that were said back then, if some outsider had overheard, would have sounded cruel, but it was happening, we had to face it, we had to deal with it.

SHAWN: The thing that bothers me is being afraid of dying, but you don't have to die. Lots of people get through cancer. I try to think I'm not going to die. But it's not bad dying 'cause you go to Heaven. The reason we're afraid of going to Heaven is 'cause we've never been there. It's like when your mom had you, you didn't want to get out in the big world, but once you're out in the big world, you don't want to leave. When you're in your mom's stomach, you don't want to leave. Everyone has to die once. Your mom'll be there soon, your brother, your sister. It's not so bad to die once in a while. You can meet your grandmother, your great-

grandmother. I would watch my grandchildren. Before I was sick I didn't think about dying. When I was sick I thought more and got scareder.

MARIA: Once Dr. Pitel saw that Shawn was more stable — he was beginning to produce platelets, he was not as dependent on transfusions — Pitel said, "Ten days of camp? Of course, send him." He never mentioned the word *remission* then, but Shawn was getting stable, something was happening. He would say, "I don't know what's going on. But whatever we're doing, let's keep on doing it." And Shawn just started picking up, a little bit, just like a little flower. Opening up.

IVONNE: I went away before Shawn went to camp, and I had never really dealt with the fact that maybe he was going to die. I went to visit my best friend because she had moved to Mississippi. And we went to the mall one day. She was getting a bathing suit and I went and picked out this black skirt and this white blouse. I bought it, and she didn't really say anything to me because my attitude was, you know, "Don't you like it?" The white blouse was so pretty, it had a little trim of lace. It was elegant. And the skirt was plain black, and I picked out these black shoes and went home and put my bag somewhere and we went out to the beach. And we were sitting there on the beach talking, and Dani asked, "Why did you buy that?" and I was, like, "What?"

"Why did you buy that skirt, that blouse?" I went back inside and I said, "God, Dani, why *did* I get that? I guess I got it for a funeral or something." So I went back the next day and returned it. And I got a bathing suit instead. I got a nice yellow polka-dot bikini.

MARIA: When no one can give me answers, I go back to my beliefs I had as a child. I grew up in Peru and I went to a Catholic school for twelve years of my life and I went to Mass every day. They taught us to love the Virgin Mary, God, and Jesus, and I remember praying in the chapel at school, every day. I would look at the Virgin and think she was *my* mother and now, this many years later, I gave Shawn to her and said, "I'm not going to fight you. This is not my baby anymore, it's yours. You're going to take care of him because I have already done everything that I could." The doctors are telling me, "There's nothing else that we can do for Shawn, we're sorry . . . ," and you feel so helpless and you're thinking, "Well, what else can I do?" All I have heard all my life is what my Catholic faith tells me: He'll go to a better place, he'll go to Heaven. I started believing that the Virgin is going to take care of him.

I guess camp gave the same kind of peace to Shawn; in his little mind probably he was saying, "Someone else is taking care of all of this, I'm fine, I'm okay, I'm going to make it." The unknown isn't scary anymore when we are certain that what is next is wonderful.

I don't want to say that believing in the Virgin is like believing in Tadger, you understand, but I'm saying, "Here, it's yours, I'm not going to fight you. You can take care of him from now on because it brings me peace."

SHAWN: The first day I got to camp I felt sad and I was scared. I missedmy mom. When I got there I just wanted to stay with my girlfriend, Ally; she's fourteen. Then I found out what unit I was in and I went there and I drawed pictures and then we got to know each other. I brought Oreos and Pringles to camp because I was afraid there wasn't going to be enough food there. Prednisone made me really hungry, so I ate 174 Oreos at camp, I added them up in the package. Oreos were the only thing I didn't like to share. The food at camp was really good. The spaghetti was my favorite. The best part of camp was woodshop. I made two Shawn signs, a heart for my mom, a rabbit for Terry, and a rabbit for Ivonne. At camp one of my friends was Tadger. He's shy and friendly and lives in the woods. He doesn't want us to see him, but I imagine he looks like a brown bear with a black nose. If you wrote letters to him, he wrote back. I asked him questions and he wrote answers back. I got the award for writing the most letters to Tadger. I wish I could see Tadger, but I understand why he is shy. He has a brother, Huggy Bear, that you can see. Huggy Bear gives me hugs.

When I was at camp I wrote some poems and I thought it was fun the first time so I went back. I had never written a poem before that. It was good expressing your feelings to the poem and to everybody who reads it.

Sometimes it's hard trying to find the right words to describe the thing that you want to talk about. I didn't put the feelings in the poems. Sometimes, you'd write the poem and you didn't know what feeling it had when it ends. Some of the poems I wrote there make me feel sad now.

Dear Mr. Leaf

I'm sorry I ripped you
I know it felt bad
but I have been through worser things than that
I just want to get it over with.

Joel's Jacket

"Oh, Joel's jacket, why are
you gray and your arms too long
for me?"
    "Because Joel picked me out
and he's big and you're small.
But I cover you almost to your legs."

Poor Dead Plant

Poor dead plant
silently dead.
You're beautiful
because you still have your leaves
and nobody chopped you down.

SHAWN: Sometimes, if you tell what you feel instead of leaving your feelings inside, it's better. If you leave them inside, you get angry, you feel like you're gonna explode. Sometimes it feels more better to tell people how you feel and what you've gone through. It's like there's a bomb inside. When there's one second left, you express your feelings and you feel better. The only person I told how I feel was my mom and my dad, Terry. I talked to Paula, too. The more people you tell, the more it helps you forget. Most of the time you tell lots of people, and when you can stop telling people, you feel better.

JEFF (Shawn's camp counselor): One day I was really stressed out and I was sitting in the bed across from Shawn's during rest hour. He got out of his bed, sensing something was wrong, said, "I love you," and kissed me on the nose. Then he put his hand on my forehead and took me through one of the meditations from his tapes. It blew me away. For a minute I was thinking, "Okay, who is who in this relationship?"

SHAWN: After I got back from camp, I was in remission. Remission, it was excellent news! It was the third time I'd been in remission. The doctors said it was the prednisone. I said Tadger had cured me with all his love and being at camp with all the love and fun, not the prednisone. The way love and fun makes you better is, say you have a stomachache and then you have some fun — all of a sudden you forget about it and you're cured. And if someone loves you so much, you forget about what you had. I like to think about how Tadger made me better. At camp I saw other people loving, and most of them loved me. I wrote these poems at camp, too; they make me feel happy.

A nice alligator, he doesn't eat anything.
He can stay alive for ten weeks, then he dies,
Comes back to life again, dies, comes back to life.

He's kind, he's playful. He plays with the fish,
The turtles. They play basketball. He looks like
A regular alligator but he has a smile all the time.
> He's a rainbow color.

The Lake

The lake wishes to be beautiful
Because it has the sun.
It wishes not to get polluted
It's afraid of being wasted.
It keeps animals alive,
Gives us something to wash with.
When someone boats through the lake
It feels special because it's being used.
He hates motorboats the most.
He likes canoes the best because he gets to see them.
He likes all the children the best and he likes goldfish
Because they make him look gold.
The ripples make the lake go
Any way they want.

This Tree Branch

Why are you brown, tree branch?
Because I am old
And when you are old you grow weak and die
But I am still alive.

Hi Tadger,

Is it all right if I share my feelings with you because there is nobody to share my feelings with? Camp is great. I wish I could see you. I have seen your brother, Huggy Bear. I like your brother. I am seven. How old are you? When is your birthday? I love you. I have so much to tell you.

Love,
Shawn

P.S. Write me back.

Dear Tadger,

If you don't know when your birthday is, ask your mom. If your brother is jealous of me, he can write me a letter. Will we ever see you? I love you. I really believe in you because I like to believe in things like that.

Love,
Shawn

MARIA: When he got back, he was a different boy. I saw a round face, a happy face. He had an aura around him of happiness and, I don't know, he was completely different. We thought: "Gosh, this is unbelievable. Four weeks ago this kid wasn't going to make it, and look at him now." He was so light, so full of life, of love, and that lasted for quite a long time.

The big question in my mind was what did Shawn know about dying? I wanted to be able to talk to him, but I had no idea what he knew. I didn't want to tell him something completely out of his scope. But when he came back from camp, at the airport, Paula told me, "You have to read the poems. They are in Shawn's suitcase." So, as soon as I got to the house, I got them out. I couldn't believe them. Those poems told me a lot of what he already knew was going on. I said, "These are wonderful, Shawn."

"Yeah, those are my poems."

I knew he had trouble with his writing so I asked, "How did you write them?"

"I just talked to Dahlia and Larry and they write it down."

"Is it something that just comes out?"

"Yeah."

But they were a big surprise for me. I don't think he would have ever been able to tell me what he was feeling. Writing, and telling someone who was not Mummy or Daddy or brother or sister and who wasn't going to start crying, seeing that for him was scary, too. It was wonderful, like therapy, something out of him.

The one about the alligator, the way I interpret it, there was no end, there were going to be some relapses but there is no end. He plays happily ever after. Paula told me: "Listen to him, don't worry, just listen to him."

DR. PITEL: We did a marrow on him when he got back from camp and he was in remission. Well, I've got to just tell you, that's a preposterous set of events. Nobody in their right mind would be *stupid* enough to try to put somebody with T-cell leukemia — in their second bone marrow relapse, after a bone marrow transplant — into remission using prednisone alone. It's *so* stupid, you'd never even consider it.

I will Sing Life

TERRY: They called me and I came to the hospital, everyone was dancing around and yelling, everybody all happy, and I walked in and Pitel is just jumping up and yelling, "Look at this!" pointing at a microscope, "Look in there!" and it's like a little kid's kaleidoscope.

MARIA: Dr. Pitel was trying to share whatever he was seeing, even if we couldn't understand. He kept saying, "Maria, sit down, you have to look!" I never look at slides of cells, so I had no idea. Dr. Pitel called the other doctor in and he kept on yelling, "Look at this kid! His marrow is completely clean! He's in remission with just prednisone."

DR. PITEL: I always joke that it was the priest's doing and I wouldn't take the credit.

MARIA: I do believe it is a miracle. A miracle that is a combination of everything: Shawn's mind, maybe a little bit of prednisone, and also the love that everybody has given him and he gives back. When he came back from camp, he wrote a letter to each of his counselors and stuffed the envelopes with seashells from Florida that he'd picked up on the beach.

PAULA: There are many of those kids that go through the same thing and everybody wants to give up on them and everybody gets into this big drama that they're going to die and they call hospice in, and then all of a sudden once they work through all the emotional stuff, they start getting better.

I knew there was a very specific reason for Shawn to be at that camp — because we all tend to know what we need inside. I always tell the children that they know what's going on. You just have to ask the part of you that knows what's going on, what you can do to get better. Shawn needed a place to feel loved, and a place to express his feelings and just be a kid.

TERRY: I think his attitude had everything to do with it. I think it has to do with the strength of his own mind. I've always said that Shawn didn't die because nobody told him he was supposed to. He went through all the motions, but nobody said to him, "You're gonna die," so he just forgot to, or never knew he was supposed to. I really feel that if we had told him, he probably would have. In fact, when the woman from the hospice program would come to our house, Shawn would get real upset. He didn't even know what she did, but he wouldn't let her touch him.

IVONNE: It's weird because it's unexplainable. It's like a miracle, but then again you don't want to accept it as a miracle because I know miracles don't happen — not in this world. It's like he's healed himself and then again, God, I don't know if I can say stuff like that. Maybe God did it, but I don't know. My mom says it's a miracle. A lot of people see it that way; they say it was because of our family. My family seems so typical at times, and I guess other people see it as so amazing and different. But it's really just loving and hugging.

J.P.: I think I bopped him on the head too much and it made him better. Yeah, probably so.

TERRY: Everyone else seemed to be extremely happy about the remission. I saw that as a big confusion. The last time was so final — "There's nothing else we can do, absolutely not, maximum thirty days." Then he's back in remission?

   And I thought, "What in the hell is everybody so happy about? What do we do now?" They said, "He's in remission. That means there's a lot of other options."

   "Well, explain those to me."

   "We could go for a second bone marrow transplant."

   That's when I asked about the radiation. You can only receive a certain amount of radiation in your lifetime, and Shawn's pretty damn close to that, and a bone marrow transplant is not that successful unless you have total body radiation. I didn't know what everyone was so happy about and I don't think they did either, other than the fact that something different had happened.

DR. PITEL: If he's out of the woods now, there's no precedent for it. But I don't like to think about it. That's *my* defense. I just play with it. Give him more leucovorin here, play with the trivia. I can't even think about it. Shawn's a really neat kid. Shawn's one of my favorites. A few weeks ago, Maria came in and she said, "How are we going to treat him?" and I got real upset. "You're not supposed to ask me that question. I don't want to think about that question." I

I Will Sing Life

don't know why it's working now. As soon as I put together a thing that goes on for one and a half or two years, it's going to all fall apart, so don't ask me to do that. I know what works for him and I know what doesn't make him sick. We're just sort of playing with it. I say to Maria, "Ask me what I'm going to do next week, don't ask me what I'm going to do in a month. I don't know what I'm going to do in a month." It's neat because it shouldn't be working at all. I mean, here's this kid who's running around, basically a perfectly healthy seven-year-old, when he shouldn't be around at all.

J.P.: I worry about him all the time. I worry when I play with him that I might punch him in his catheter. Me and Lee wrote this poem about him:

Kite

Eagle,
The golden sun,
Fast as a fox,
Sometimes, slow as an ant.
You get to fly.
Freedom is all colors.
Freedom smells like fresh cut grass.
Freedom feels good like the foggy mornings when we had coffee at
        the Jiffy, just the two of us.
You get to stay up in the air,
But you can't stay forever,
And you get holes in you.
Controlled by a string,
Sad because you're not free.
Something special in the air,
But when you crash, nobody,
Crash like somebody dropped a jackknife out of an airplane,
All broken in pieces,
Twirling like a fan.
Like a broken wing on a bird.
The ground is the kite's doctor, it rests there.
Our bird kites would help you.
They'd stick out a wing and wing you up.

Our bird kites could come off their strings any time,
But they are waiting for you to get better,
So they can cut your string so you can fly off, too.
— LEE DUGGER AND J. P. VALDEZ

MISS O: Somebody in our class once asked, "Will Shawn go to third
    grade?" And I said, "What do you think?"
        "Does he have to get real well to go to third grade?"
        "No. He can go to third grade and he can take a nap every day."
        "But what if he gets real, real sick and he has to go to the
    hospital? Would he go to third grade?"
        "Sure, because he'll get a teacher to come to his house."
        "And will that make him ready to go to third grade?"
        "Yes, because Shawn is smart."
        But I know the underlying question is, "Will Shawn be
    around to go to third grade?"
        Everybody just mothers him. And I don't think I've said to

them, "You need to mother Shawn." But they mother him, get his lunch, give him their jacket, hold his hand . . .

SHAWN: One of the things I hate the most is when I get V.G.s [Very Goods] at school and I don't deserve them. And it makes me mad when they pretend they can't catch me when we play tag, because I know they can.

JANET: I wouldn't like anybody to laugh at Shawn. He's the only one who's a little bit littler than the other kids, so we should be nice to him. He can't really run that fast, so we pretend we can't really run that fast and play with him. We pretend to be pushing him down and then he fights us back with his Ninja Turtle things. He knows we're just pretending. He likes it.

It's hard because no one really tells me what's wrong with Shawn. I know that cancer's not a really good thing to have. I would love it if I could tell his mom things about what I don't understand and I wish she'd tell me. Like, where's the hospital? And why does Shawn always go away? Like, why does he always go to sleep? I don't understand that. He always feels a little bit drowsy and I don't know why. He doesn't want anyone to notice that he doesn't have any hair. But you CAN notice that.

In our class, I watch Shawn the most. Me and Miss O. There's lots of stuff we learn that Shawn can't do yet. Like math things. Sometimes on tests he gets like minus one and things, sometimes he gets minus sixteen. That's not really good. We want him to learn everything right. So what are we gonna do? I worry that he might not get to go to third grade. 'Cause if he's just in second grade all the time, what would he learn? Would he learn how to do cursive?

IVONNE: It's like he's in limbo now, and at times, like when I'm helping him with his homework and he doesn't want to do it and I'm, like, "Shawn, you have to. You have to pass second grade and go to third grade and fourth grade and fifth grade." And as I'm saying this, I'm thinking, "Yeah." There's always the chance that he won't be there. Sometimes I yell at him, because you have to be stern with him. But later I'm thinking, "God, you just yelled at him. What if that's the last thing that's been said?" But that's not good. I don't like that feeling to be there. Right now we no longer live in the past or in the future. It's day by day. If he goes tomorrow, he goes tomorrow, just be thankful to have him here today. Like Shawn, he just concentrates on playing, and doing his own thing and not really talking about it or dealing with it.

J.P.: Shawn doesn't want to remember stuff that happened a long time ago. I guess that's because he just wants to play video games.

PAULA: There's that little place that we all have where we stick all the stuff we don't really want to talk about. We cover it up and just say it's not there because it's too frightening to look at. A lot of this stuff he won't discuss because it's too much to handle at one time. It'll just come out in other conversations, or in his poems, or when he plays.

The Leukemia Game (for Nintendo)

The bad guys would be the leukemia cells. They would look disgusting. They would have nasty weapons: spears, boomerangs, and ninja stars. And then there are these good guys that would help me. They would be the red cells, the white cells, and me. The red cells could power you up. The white cells would give you a new weapon or you could find a weapon under a bone. You could put up a calendar. The calendar can help you because you only have a few days. You could show it one of the days of the month, like Valentine's Day. The leukemia cell is a slimy guy. You can show him the calendar and he'll keep on staring at it and get smaller and smaller and get locked up in a tiny cage in the date. You could use it as a weapon, too, you could swing it at somebody.

When you get poisoned by the leukemia cells, you can go to an inn that restores your life, like a clinic. They will ask you for some money, some gold, which you can find along the way. Chemo is a thing that you really need in the clinic if you get poisoned by a bad cell. At first you have your hair, but when you get poisoned, you lose it. At the clinic they give you a hat for free and your hair grows back as you're playing. Sometimes you need a spinal tap for a different kind of poison. You wait in a room, see a doctor, see an I.V. so you can go to sleep. Then the screen darkens while they do the spinal tap because you're asleep. Then the light goes on and you go down the elevator. Sometimes when the leukemia cells hit you, they hit you really bad but you can go to the clinic for a bone marrow. A bone marrow is like chemo, but all your power gets refilled. For a bone marrow transplant they check my family to see if they match. They have to get a shot and you see a tube with stuff in it that's red. The doctor holds two tubes and when they look the same, they match. After your treatment it blinks on and off and your power is all refilled.

To kill the leukemia cells, you have to find potions in these villages. The potions give you spells. One of the spells is Fun. You chant it to all the leukemia cells and they have fun and forget about their job. Another spell is Friends. All the platelets come up and they become friends with the bad cells. Another spell is called Forgetting, that makes the bad guys forget and they just walk away. Then they die in a poof of smoke. There is a spell called Family, that restores energy and magic and helps you move faster. The last spell is called Dance. Everybody dances and as soon as the bad cells dance, they blow up. They dance to New Kids on the Block.

At the end of each stage there is a boss. At the final stage you see the Leukemia Boss, he looks kind of like a tomato, but shaped like a heart. He bumps. There are wires that are hooked up to him and you have to cut them off. When he dies, he goes, "Gggggggg . . ."

The Squirrel

Up in a big tree is a squirrel that had cancer and he wished he could be cured and he got cured. He has a telephone inside the tree, his dad helped him get it there with a ladder. In his room he has a bed, he has clothes. He's a messy squirrel. His clothes are on the floor. He is wearing a white T-shirt with a picture of three squirrels skating. He has a little desk for the white phone. He calls all the other squirrels who have cancer. They are scared about having cancer. He tells them not to be scared and to be happy searching for peanuts, and whoever got the most would win, and running races, and hide and seek. They forgot all about having cancer and they think about just keeping their mind on the game.

Wish Poem

If I could have three wishes
I would wish that there was no polluting.
I would wish that there were no weapons.
I would wish to have 500 dollars.
I would give each of my 100 dollars
To my sister, my brother, my mom, my dad, and Lee.

IVONNE: My mother has this incredible faith in God; it's unreal. Like, I
can remember when Shawn relapsed, the last time, we were going
to the mall to get shoes or something. We started talking about my
grandmother who had passed away a while ago. My mother was
talking about how wonderful it was, that if Shawn was to go away,
that he'd be up there with my grandmother. And I was just thinking, "God, Mom, how can you be so, I don't know . . . optimistic?"
But I mean, I guess that it *is* a very peaceful thought because I can

imagine both my grandmothers over there, fighting over Shawn, you know, and cooking, and it makes me smile and feel so much better about everything.

I can't imagine what it would be like when he's cured, period. My mom will talk about the future like: "I can see you coming home, all in your professional clothes, dropping your kids off, J.P. coming over and Shawn, dropping off their kids. . . ." That's such a cool way of looking at things, having Shawn there in the future.

PAULA: Nobody knows how long any of us are going to be alive, and one thing's for sure: there are lots of people in lots of places who were told that they were going to be dead very soon but they've survived for years and years. We don't hear about them because there are not a lot of studies about that. We're not taught to believe in what we can't measure, what can't be seen. Do you see anybody doing research on miracles? No. All you see is research on people that die. So I tell the kids I work with: "I'm here to tell you that I know this person, this person, and this person who are miracles, and these are people in *your* clinic. There's no such thing as false hope, and in the face of uncertainty, hope is okay. So let's just believe in something great, let's believe in a miracle."

MARIA: I'm experiencing a miracle right now and I remind myself every minute of it, every time I see his little face and his little smile. I can see he's my walking miracle. And I feel very, very special. He has a purpose. I take it as a temporary miracle. I don't want to look at it like it's a permanent miracle. That's only up to God. To me, that's why having him singing in the choir in church this Christmas, I was the happiest woman in the whole world. After almost two years of suffering, I feel that no matter what happens now, no matter what happens, he's shown everybody so much, having faith.

It is wonderful because before Shawn ever got sick — your normal daily life falls into a routine, especially when you have little ones around. I've always been a working mother, so you go to work, come home, take care of them, and think: "When are these boys going to grow? When are they going to behave?" You're a little bit frustrated about the whole thing. I always loved my children, but it seems like with all of this I see life and I see them growing in such special ways. I'm enjoying every minute of it.

My baby was not supposed to be here with me anymore. But he is still here. Let's make it happy. We're not going to be here forever. You get patience from nowhere. It's like we were living in a black-and-white picture and then suddenly a fairy godmother came and colored it, and it's wonderful. It's good to be able to enjoy life again because before, daily things, Shawn being sick, and his treatment and going to the clinic and the doctors, took probably 200 percent of my energy and I was hurting inside because I knew the rest of my family, the rest of the people who cared about me, were hurting too because I was not able to give them the love and attention that I should. They understood, of course, but you know, I knew I was neglecting Ivonne. And I was seeing a little bit of stuff going on with J.P. That hurt me a lot.

Funny, but with Terry and me, our relationship was getting stronger and stronger. Having Terry with me is what has given me strength, having his love and acceptance. Not having to worry about a lot of little things, no, very important things like who's going to pay the mortgage. I had to go to Gainesville for two months for the transplant. I had to quit work. What do I do if the car breaks down? What do I do with the rest of the kids if I have to run to the hospital in the middle of the night? There were many many times — you can be strong to a point — when you ask, "Why? I don't want to live like this anymore." And you just fall over completely or you cry and scream and then he would be holding me and then suddenly everything comes back to normal. Now Shawn is doing fine, Ivonne is coping with all of this, I have been able to spend time with J.P. and Lee. It's wonderful to be able to get up in the morning and not have to worry about running to the hospital. Just feed the children breakfast, put them to bed at night, plan weekends.

At this moment I just thank God for everything I have. I just thank Him for everything. I don't pray for Him to . . . I don't say, "God, please don't let him relapse." No. Not anymore. Just, "Thank you, God."

I Will Sing Life

Dear Tadger,

On Halloween I was a Ninja Turtle, I was Michelangelo. I miss you. I'm coming back to camp. I hope you can come out but you don't have to if you don't want to. I hope one day I can see what you are.

Love
Your Friend, Shawn

P.S. My mom sends her love.

Joe Lopez

JOE DOES NOT have plans to be a boxer like his father and grandfather before him, but he still plans to fight. He lives in a neighborhood where some of his twelve-year-old classmates are in gangs and where fights break out every day after school. Joe faces much tougher opponents than the other kids. As one of the oldest children in the country born HIV positive, he fights statistics that say he might not live to be a teenager. He has twice defeated the pneumonia that kills most children with AIDS.

He also combats a prejudice that says he must fight alone. Joe has had to hold back the impulse to tell people about his disease. He knows about the attacks on other kids who have said publicly that they have AIDS; he knows how Ryan White's grave has been repeatedly desecrated. Still, when we told Joe he should write his chapter without his real name or photograph, he refused. He insisted that this was his chance to use the facts to fight prejudice, and that Joe Lopez is one fact he is willing to fight for.

MOST children who have gone public were infected by a blood transfusion. Joe, however, speaks for a silent majority of kids born to mothers who have shared contaminated drug needles. Joe is ready to challenge anyone who says that there is something bad about him because of where his disease came from.

His toughest opponent, however, is one that has never been defeated. Every day, Joe fights the AIDS virus itself — it has taken on an identity and life in his imagination. He fights it in his poems, in his drawings, and in the games he plays. Then he fights it again in his dreams at night.

Unlike the children who can dream of defeating their opponent, Joe dreams only of fighting. He does not imagine final victory, but neither does he imagine surrender.

WHEN kids at school ask why I go to clinic every month, I tell them I've got cancer. If they ask me where's my mom, I tell them that she's dead. Like this girl was cheating in a game, and I said, "Don't cheat, don't cheat," and she said, "You better mind your business. Go mind your mother's business," and I said, "I can't mind my mother's business because she's in Heaven." She said, "How'd she die?" and I said, "I don't know, cancer." My friends ask me and they know I'm lying, because when I'm lying I talk low. This book is the first time I had a choice. I didn't have to use my real name in it but I wanted to. Because I'm sick and tired of holding it in. I want everybody to know who I was.

My real name is Joe Louis Lopez. If they change my name, then it's not me, it's somebody else. But it *is* me. It's a fact. People are afraid of AIDS and you have to show them they're wrong by telling them to read, get their facts right. When I give out the facts about me, people might think, "Oh, get away from him, he has AIDS," but I don't care what they think. It's what I think inside and what my family thinks — my dad, my brothers, and my stepmom, Susan.

At school, I told five kids about having it after I got to know them real good and they didn't say nothing. I told my best friends Mario, Eddie, Robert, Christian, and Bruce. I let them into my house to eat lunch and they said, "How'd your mom die?" and I told them, "By AIDS," and they said, "Oh. Were you inside of her when she had it?" and I said, "Yeah, but I don't know if I have it." Then I said, "Yeah, I do have it. Don't do anything stupid." They said, "No, we wouldn't." They didn't get scared, they just said, "I understand, don't worry about it," and they stayed my best friends.

I will Sing Life

Hiding

I hide love in my heart
and let it out when I think it's the right girl.
I hide secrets in my pocket
where it's cold and deep,
and when they tell me I can tell someone,
I let the secrets out.
I hide my feelings in a swamp
where no one can find it
and in my brain and my journal.
I hide a beaver dam in my blood,
when the virus comes the beaver
slaps him with his tail.
I hide a bird in my stomach,
when he is hungry he will growl.
I will hide myself inside of a bear,
so everyone will be scared of me.
I will eat fish every day and berries and honey.
I hide inside my dream
to seek feelings that I don't even know.

I know how to box, 'cause my father was a boxer. He won the Golden Gloves. My grandfather did too. I saw my father box. He quit because of my real mom, when she was having me.

My dad taught me to stand, like you wouldn't be able to sweep me, unless you bring your knee in and push me down. Want to see some steps? "One, two, one, two, uppercut." My name would be, lemme see . . . Thunderbolt Lopez. Or Lightning Lopez. When I'm in the shower, I fight the water, because it's hard and you can't move fast. "Lightning Lopez against Waterfall Tyson." It's hard because I slap the water and it comes back to me. I beat him up and I say: "The winner, Champion of the World, Lightning Lopez!!"

I'd like to have a talk show for kids with diseases, and not that corny stuff about people that died and went to Heaven and met the earth angels. On my show, we'd talk about more important things, but I won't get into their business. I'd ask, "How long you had it?" but not "How'd you get it?" or stupid stuff like that. I can talk about how I got it, but sometimes, with strangers, I don't like to.

I got it because my real mom used to do drugs. She didn't realize it,

though. It makes me mad that she died and stuff, but it's not her fault. Not
her fault. I used to get mad because my mom knew about doing drugs and
she still did it. I wish she would have stopped and I wish she would have
found out if she had it or not. When I was mad, I said all kind of things.
But I remember my mom real well, she would always protect me, no matter what. Like when I played hooky once with my brother, and my father
found out, she said, "No no, it's because I took him to the doctor." She
stuck up for me. She said, "You better not do that again," and I never did.
From that day on I never played hooky.

Back then I didn't know what AIDS was. I thought it was "Eggs." The
first time I heard about AIDS was when I was six. I didn't know my mom
was sick until she went into the hospital. She came out in a month but
then she got sick again and went to the hospital again. I saw her in the
hospital on a Saturday morning and then every week I saw her on the
same day. She was pale and she was shaking, and I asked, "How come
she's dying?" My father said, " 'Cause she has AIDS," and that's when I
found out what it was about. The last time I saw her my father picked me
up because my mother was dying and he wanted me to see her before she

died. I wanted to tell her that I loved her, and she told my father that her last request was "take care of my son." She told me, "I love you." The next morning my grandfather came and said my mother died at six o'clock in the morning. Me and my brother Charles started crying when we found out. Charlie was mad, because she died. She was young. She was only twenty-nine. He don't think about it that much, 'cause if he does, his feelings will come back. Charlie is seventeen. He's my real mom's son, before she got AIDS, but not my dad's, and he's not HIV. I have a little baby brother, Matthew, who's almost two. He's Susan and my dad's son, and they're not HIV so he's not either. When Susie was pregnant, I told her not to smoke or drink, 'cause I didn't want him to get sick, and she quit. He's really big and smart. I like having a baby brother. I learned how to feed him and how to change diapers because I practiced on a stuffed animal.

NOBODY knew I had it until a week after my mom died, when I went into the hospital. I had seizures and high fevers from the HIV when I was a baby, but the doctors didn't know what HIV was then. Then I got sick from pneumonia when I was six, and they told my dad and Susie what I had. My social worker, Mary, she told them that they should tell me. My father and Susie didn't want to keep nothing from me, so they told me. Lots of kids, their parents don't tell them that they have AIDS. I think they should know because otherwise they find out the hard way, because the family knows, and someone gets mad and says, "You got AIDS!" That's not the right way to find out.

My dad and Susie just said, "Joe, lay down," 'cause I was sitting down eating my breakfast. I said, "But I'm hungry!" and they said, "You know why you're in the hospital?" and I said, "Yeah, because I have pneumonia," and they said, "No, because you have HIV, that's what Mommy had." And I said, "Oh, that's nice." I didn't know what it was. Then I said, "I have Eggs? EGGS?" And they said, "No, no, AIDS," and I said, "Yeah, Eggs!" 'cause I couldn't pronounce it, and they started laughing and from then on, I knew what it was.

PEOPLE are scared of AIDS because they don't have the facts, they think you can get it just by touching a person. Like Ryan White. He was about my age and he went to a school and they found out and they kicked him out of school and he had to go to court for that. People should know that you can't get AIDS from swimming in the same pool, or getting a mosquito bite, or sharing cigarettes, or kissing. Some people say that someone with AIDS would look like a bum or someone who doesn't have money, or

uses it all on drugs. People with AIDS look ordinary, like you and me. You can get AIDS through birth, sex with a person infected with HIV, transfusions, drugs, and that's it. Or when you shoot drugs, if you don't clean the needle and use the same one as somebody who has AIDS. People think that drugs make them feel good but they don't know what they are doing to themselves. Drugs don't only kill your brain, they infect your body. If your mom has it, you get it . . . and when you got it, that's the end. No cure. It's like a birthmark. It will never go away.

I think it sucks that you never hear on the news that a person *lives* with AIDS. You always hear that someone died last night. But HIV is nothing, it's just a virus. It's just like being sick for a long time, for always. You can have HIV for many years and not be sick. But you can die from AIDS in a second. HIV is the name of AIDS as a virus, and when HIV makes you very sick, you've got full-blown AIDS. The virus attacks your immune system and it kills your white cells that fight viruses. You have to take care of yourself or you could get HIV pneumonia. I say, put on your gloves and fight 'em, go ten rounds. You have to beat it. But some people, they're scared, they just say, "Nah, I can't beat it, I can't." They don't care about themselves because they think they're dying. I got nothing to talk about dying. I ain't dying yet.

I only go to clinic once a month. I started going when I was seven. I didn't even know what it was. At first I didn't like the needles and stuff. The needles are for taking blood, and they give you chicken pox and measles needles. They weigh you and make sure you're gaining weight. I'm losing weight even though I'm eating all the time, because of the HIV. If I lose weight, they have to put me in the hospital and put tubes in my nose and Susie don't want to see that. If I get virus pneumonia again, I'll stay in the hospital for like a month. HIV pneumonia is the baddest pneumonia you would ever want. When I had it, I was real sick, I had a high fever the whole time. They put an I.V. into me, and kept me in the hospital until I was cured. Now, every time I get sick my father says, "Oh, you have to take care of yourself, I don't want you to die now." That's stupid, I'm not gonna die just because I get a cold or something. It makes me mad that he worries like that. But I like it sometimes. Susie gets mad at me for not taking care of myself and she gets mad at my dad for treating me like I'm gonna die. Yesterday, for Susie, I made "Mom" and then I put words into the M, O, and M. Like on the first 'M' I put "Mostly terrific" and on the 'O' I put awesome.

Once, when I was little, Mary, my social worker, caught me eating spinach and asparagus and I never liked them and she said, "How come you're eating that?" and I said, "Because I wanna live. I don't wanna die like my mom. She was stupid for dying." Then she said, "Well, you don't have to eat that." And after that I never ate it again. My mom used to say, "You want to be like Popeye?" and I said, "Yeah, I want to be strong," and she said, "Eat your spinach," and I ate it. Now I know how to take care of myself. Eat healthy food, sleep, keep exercising, take my medicine. I take AZT four times a day. It tastes like cement. It makes you eat better and helps you not to get sick. You should never miss a dose. Missing a dose is like missing a second of your life.

AZT isn't a cure, it's just something that slows AIDS down. They won't have a cure until 2000, that's what doctors on the news say, but I don't know if it's true. If they were trying their best, it would be soon, but they're not. Because AZT came up fast, but after that nothing else came up.

A Cure for HIV and AIDS

My wish is to find a cure for AIDS.
I hope it's a mysterious lollipop because I'm sick of
All these medicines, or maybe even an icepop,
Maybe something even more terrific:
Just wake up one morning and not have it.

Now I'm the lollipop
First thing I would do as the lollipop,
I would seek and destroy the virus
Make sure there's no survivors,
When I suck the lollipop, the juices put it into a trance.

Now I'm the icepop.
First thing I would do as the icepop is
Freeze the bad feeling.
I would find it, put a spring freeze on it and smash it.

Bad feelings look like a dog
That just got swiped by a car.
The good feelings look like a baby turtle.
I would melt the bad feelings, so the good feelings can flow.

I will Sing Life

You have to challenge AIDS, beat it in your dreams and wake up the next morning and maybe it won't be there. I can control some things with my head. Sometimes, like when I feel I have a stomachache, I control it and I don't go to the nurse. Or, if I'm having a happy dream and a nightmare comes in, I control it. I pretend I'm a martial artist and a ninja. I jump off the wall and flip and get them under my power and then I wake up. In my dreams, I fight everybody. I fight Cyclops, the dude with one eye. I read about him.

I DO combat against my virus. Sometimes I go into my body and I fight my cells and I defeat them. They are red, blue, and every color. They have eight legs or seven legs that have claws at the end. I use a slingshot. I put white cells on them and "*whishhh*," and red cells on them, "*whishhh*." I would wear one of them old days things like He Man wears, and Rambo, tight shorts, and a machine gun, a slingshot. I kill them all. When they die, my disease is cured. I didn't get to the leader yet in my dreams, but I know he'll have a hard shell with spikes on it, big claws, and boxing gloves. He'll have every kind of weapon you could think of, machine guns, bazooka, power pack, all kinds of guns, radioactive waves, everything. When I do find the leader, I'm gonna wrap my boomerang with rope and wrap it around his leg and tie him up, and give him everything I got. When I kill him, that will cure it in real life. I started a secret club, called the D-Force, with Dahlia and Larry. We fight the AIDS virus. This is what I wrote about it:

The D Force

MISSION: To seek every bad disease and destroy it. Find it, trick it, and then blast it because it is disgusting to think about it.

ENEMY NAME: AIDS

CODE NAME: HIV

LOCATION: The human body.

HISTORY: His hiding place is inside the human body. When the human body finds it, he finds the best medicine and destroys the virus, but the virus has babies. He gets you when you are sleeping, he gets you when you are awake. If you got a cut he'll get you then. He gets into your blood and he'll destroy you unless you destroy him first.

WEAKNESSES: Medicines, healthy food, not using drugs, and rocking and rolling all night long. No other weaknesses.

APPEARANCE: Ugly, looks like a disgusting pig, he's got holes in his skin and his face, but when I get through with him he'll have holes all over his body.

The disease-control crimefighters are three people, one with a staff, one with a light saber, and one with magic lipstick: Darkwing, Double Dribble, and De Unknown. They always cook up a mystery and they always cook up a good dinner. Crimefighting is a hungry job, but somebody's gotta do it. They get their powers by drinking good stuff like O.J., apple cider, and eating pizza, eggs, and stuff like that. Their goal is to defeat the evil diseases, sickle cell anemia, AIDS, and cancer.

Our hideout is called DeepWoods, and the leader in command is Darkwing. We love to party and we love making booby traps in club houses and when we find those diseases, we're going to torture them and destroy them.

The End.

Things that fight become friends. That's how it goes with me. If I fight with somebody we become a team because after we fight I know they can fight good so I want them on my side. Then when I get in another fight, they will jump in. I fought Mario, and now he's my best friend. I was trying to be nice to him and tell him I cared about him, so I made his girlfriend a flower out of tissues. It was nothing big but he got jealous and he got mad at me, in front of my house. I said, "All right. Let's go." I threw my scarf down, it was in the wintertime, I threw my gloves down, *bap bap bap*. The cops came because a cop lives right next to me. I said, "I don't care," *bap bap bap,* I kept on beating him up. I gave him two black eyes, and a fat lip and now he's my best friend and we haven't had a fight since. I don't fight with my other best friend Eddie because he's bigger than me, he'd beat me up.

Poems of Love

When a mountain fights a cloud
That means they fall in love
But how do they fall in love with the clouds?
They fall in love as soon as they intersect
And it feels like a first kiss and thunder comes
Because it's their moment.

When rain fights snow it's love at first sight
Then ice appears and that's their baby.

When a plant fights a rock they
Fall in love, too, and they have a baby,
And it's the cactus.

When rain fights the sky they also fall
Water-over-clouds
In love with each other
And a heart of angels appears.

The hand fights paper and pencil
And they have an expression
As their baby.

A poem fights
A girl's heart
In ways of
LOVE.

Things that fight also fall in love. Like, before I get a girlfriend, I fight the girl. I'm a heartbreaker. I always have to let go of the girls. When they like me, I gotta tell them no because there's so many of them. I'm writing poems for the girl I like now. If she ever asks me about HIV, I'll tell her if I think she can handle it. Maybe other girls won't like me when they find out, but I'll tell my girlfriend the facts, I'll bring her books and everything and information. I'll say, "It's up to you."

Love

Love is like a wolf seeking its prey.
And if it's mad it can sometimes tear you apart.
It is hungry for its honey and wants a clean heart
If you have strong love it lasts forever.
If you have that penny love, it lasts until the rain is over
That's all I have to say. Peace Out!

I go to counseling at Children's Group once a month. There's seven kids in Group and sometimes you talk about what you think about the hospital and sometimes you just hang out. We talk about how we think of the needles, if they hurt, and we draw pictures of how it feels. I drew a big needle coming at me like a monster. Then it felt better. There was a girl who went to camp that I knew in Group, but she died last year. She was like eleven or twelve years old. I thought it was messed up because she was too young to die.

I HAVE a lot of feelings that I don't talk about. I'm mostly happy but I get mad when they plan on taking me somewhere and then they say, "No, no, we're not going." Because I get my hopes up. Grown-ups don't understand that kids are human beings just like you and me. Sometimes being sick makes me mad, like why was it me and nobody else? But I just think I'm gonna grow up. I believe that. It helps me feel better. When I grow up I wanna be a cop. That's what I wanted to be since I was able to know what a cop was. A cop or a writer. Or a writer-cop.

When I wish, I wish that I could take my baby brother to Florida and I wish there was a cure for every disease. I wish I could stay at camp all year long. I learned how to swim underwater at camp and that's how I got my bracelet, for deep water swimming. I never swimmed in deep water before. The Hole in the Wall Gang Camp's the only camp I ever went to. The best part was being in the clown show. We do a show for the camp, and we're dressed up like clowns. We get in a pretend car on our way to a place called Clownsville. We run into a lot of obstacles and we're supposed to make the audience laugh, so for trouble in the engine we take a Newman's Own lemonade carton out of the engine and say, "I knew this car was a lemon," or we take a rubber chicken out and say, "So this is what was fowling things up," and the gas we fill it with is laughing gas. When we get caught by the cops, we throw a pie in his face.

Clowns are like water
Make everyone laugh maybe
Commit a face crime

That's a haiku. I went to the poetry program at camp because everyone was watching a movie, and me and my friend wanted to do some exotic writing with Larry and Dahlia instead. I liked it a lot so I went back because I got to write about whatever I wanted to write, even the virus.

The message I want to write for everyone to hear is: Take care of yourself, or else you'll be in your grave, like my mom.

I GUESS maybe God decides who bad things happen to. He says eeny-meeny-miny-mo. Sometimes I think there's a God, sometimes I don't. When there's a miracle on TV or something, that's when I think there's a God. And when I ask for something and it don't happen, there's no God. When you pray, it don't make a difference if He's already decided about you. But if He hasn't decided yet, He might change His mind. I saw miracles like this one little baby that went into a coma and came back but she was blind, and a couple months later she could see. I saw that on Sally Jessy Raphaël. That baby deserved a miracle because she was so little. I was already old when I found out. God will answer your prayers if you deserve it, if you do what you're supposed to do and take care of yourself. I pray every night before I go to sleep. I say God bless my family and friends, and I try to say hi to my mom and to my uncle. Sometimes they talk back to me. I just think about my mom, and she's there. I ask her how she's doing, how is it up there? She says she can't tell me. But I think it's nice there, there won't be crime. She says, "How are you doing? You better do the right thing or else I'm gonna put lightning on you." Sometimes she says that.

Come with me and you shall hear and see
of the cure for every disease. You shall
find the mystery and answer that
you shall know.
The cure is to find the master of disease, which is yourself.
Their secret is even though you try to defeat them,
there's no way you can.
They have a secret weapon to back them up.

Come and see with me the mystery of every girl,
the gossip they talk and exaggeration they say.
They say boys exaggerate but girls
just want to save their butt and have fun.
The secret of gossip is to lie
and make trouble spread like a bird spreads its wings.

If I'm the sky or the sun or even a bird
I'll shine light in my baby brother's window.
If I was a bird I will come down and carry away
every crook in the whole entire world.
If I was the sky and wind and sun together,
I'll blow, burn and destroy every
drug off the face of this earth.

Come and see me in the brain of a cheetah
I would tell the cheetah how fast it should go
when it's gonna attack,
and how slow it should go
when its dreaming,
and how quiet it should be
when its acting,
and how fierce it will be
when it's building a home.
Don't forget to come and see
all the wonders that I can foresee for you.

Katie Martin

DAVID WAS CRYING at the dance. He had spent most of the year in the hospital, struggling to make it to camp, and now the session was almost over. When Dahlia tried to console him, he cried, "I'm just so *sick* of being a cancer kid."

Katie wandered away from the music to where David was sitting. Because her memory is impaired, she did not know if she had ever met him, but she swung her good right arm around him anyway. She whispered, "It's okay . . . don't cry," but David would not look up. As Katie ambled off, Dahlia pointed out that Katie had survived a brain tumor and that her left side was paralyzed from a stroke. David started to cry even harder. Then he asked if Katie could come back.

"When did you get your tumor?" he asked her.

"A year ago, when I was twelve."

"I have a tumor, too. See, here's my scar."

"Cool. Mine's on the other side."

In the two quietest voices at the dance, they talked about losing their hair, about brain surgery, and about almost dying. They held each other in silence for a long time. Then, suddenly, David straightened his bandanna and asked, "Wanna dance?"

For the rest of the evening they danced, held hands, and laughed. The next day, David made Katie a wooden whistle and Katie wrote David a poem. She announced to her cabin that she was "in loooove."

The doctors say that only one-third of Katie's brain functions normally. Her short-term memory and ability to put things in sequence were severely damaged by radiation treatment and a stroke. The particulars of everyday life fade from her mind as quickly as they occur — she can rarely remember how to get to her next class at school, or what she learned in the previous class.

She is, however, able to remember things that excite her emotions or her will. She remembers all the words to her favorite songs, and anything involving gymnastics, makeup, or boys. Her mind distills life to an impassioned essence. The tumor and stroke stole two-thirds of her brain, but have intensified her self.

Katie's mother gave us the following chronology of the eight months of her illness (in her chapter, Katie offers her own, quite different recollection of these events):

In December, I took Katie to the eye doctor because she was crashing into walls and would not go on the balance beam. She started crying because she couldn't read the eye test. The doctor took me out of the room and told me that it was probably a tumor. We didn't tell Katie until January, when she had a biopsy.

The biopsy determined that the tumor was inoperable, but if it was treated by radiation, there was an eighty percent chance of recovery. She had radiation for six weeks, during which she

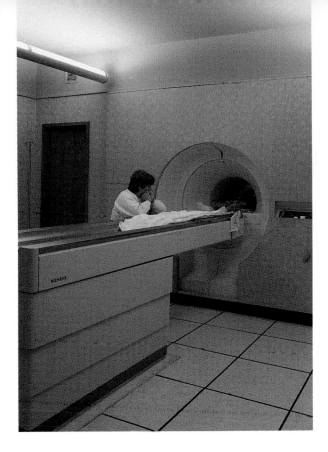

gradually lost her hair. The radiation was successful, but when we went for a routine checkup, she had to be admitted for endocrine complications. Within twenty-four hours she was having massive seizures from an electrolytic imbalance in her brain. For a few weeks she was totally wacko. She wouldn't keep her clothes on. She actually did a somersault even though her hands were tied to the bed. The doctors watched at her door in disbelief.

In April, Katie was on oxygen when all of a sudden she said, "Mommy, can I go now? Grammy's calling me." I said, "No!" and ran into the hallway. The doctors came in and all the monitors were slowing down. We thought she was dying right there. It took about five minutes to figure out that the oxygen mask was unplugged from the wall. They didn't expect her to make it.

A few days later they put her on a ventilator because she had pneumonia. She couldn't communicate at all. A social worker came in and asked: "So, have you told Katie she'll never be a gymnast again?" and all her monitors went bonkers. A few days later, Katie yanked the ventilater out. All she said was, "I'm sorry I did that, but I couldn't breathe with that damn thing in."

One day when I went in to visit her, I lifted up her arm and it just dropped and I saw her face sagging and I realized she must have had a stroke. The steroids and radiation had weakened her blood vessels. They said the next three days were touch and go and we could lose her.

In May she started rehabilitation for the stroke. Although they said she would never walk and might not talk again, two months later she was discharged from the hospital in a wheelchair, but able to talk. Then in August, only eight months after her tumor was first diagnosed, Katie went to camp.

At camp that summer, we took Katie out in a canoe. The sky was blue and full of white swelling clouds about which Katie immediately wanted to write poems. Katie watches the whole world in a way that most people watch clouds — each drifting moment is more vivid and beautiful because it will disappear without a trace.

Katie's poetry arises not only out of what she forgets, but also out of the intensity of what remains within her. Katie brings a deep compassion to everyone she sees and everything she does. The clouds in the poem she wrote watch over people on earth and cheer them up. It is this compassion that enables her to conclude her chapter with so powerful a memory.

Peaceful Adventures

I am peaceful and quiet.
There is a sound in the distance.
I have too many peaceful moments.
Before I was sick, I had more adventure moments.
In a windstorm, or a rainstorm,
A tree has an adventure moment.
The tree looks like a maze or a bunch of worms.
It would be adventurous if I could climb the tree.
It could be a place for a tree house,
To look at birds and people below.
If it was a wishing tree, it would give you wishes.
I would wish to be able to do everything I did before
I had my stroke.
I would wish for really long blond hair down to my armpits.
I would brush it five times a day and wear no hairspray.
It can be really peaceful to sit and have an adventure in your mind.

I want this chapter to tell the truth of what happened to me and then end with a happy ending. I had a brain tumor and a stroke, but I'm better now. I want it to talk about boys and music. Definitely about gymnastics and all my coaches and friends. Camp and my family and boys, definitely boys.

MY real name is Katherine Louise Martin. When we lived in Alabama, my dad sometimes called me Katie Lou for a joke. And Katie Lou Martin is kind of like Mary Lou Retton. Now that I started to write poetry, I think it should be K. L. Martin because that sounds like a poet. Not Katherine Louise Martin, but short and sweet, like Shel Silverstein. I love boys. I'm looking for a boyfriend all the time. I like everything about them. Brains, athletic, likes animals. And a good kisser. You can always tell if a boy is a good kisser, but you have to kiss him first. Then they're a good kisser if they like to kiss.

I know that boys like girls who have built chests because I'm not going out with anyone and I obviously don't have a chest. Well, I do. But not a *built* chest. I'm not growing because of the brain tumor I had. It was right near my pituitary gland so I guess it stopped the flow of stuff that makes you grow. I love holding hands with boys the interlocked-fingers way, because your hearts are interlocked. It's like the seeds in a wheat plant, holding on so they won't blow away. Anyway, I guess boys are sort of scared about cancer. Mostly, they just don't want to talk about it. None of the kids at school really wants to talk about it.

RIGHT now, I'm pretty short, but when I start growth hormone shots, I'll start to grow again. They said I'll probably be normal sized. It doesn't really matter to me that I'm smaller than the other kids because I'm just me and I never have to bend down to make myself look short if I don't want to stand out in a crowd.

I CAN'T remember things very well because my brain is messed up from the radiation I had for my tumor. I remember some things, but not others. I remember words to songs really well, and things that happened a long time ago. When someone asks me and I can't remember, sometimes I make things up. I used to make up stories all the time because I couldn't remember, but then I'd forget and get caught up in them. I don't like to talk about memories. When I try to remember something and it's not there, I get a blank and it's just black, like a tree or a stone that can't think. Nothing happens. Sometimes, there are flashes. Like, music can help me remember. Sometimes it flashes right away, sometimes it takes a while. Then I see words in the flashes in my mind, in different colors and shapes and ways of writing.

SOMETIMES I can figure it out. Like, if someone asked me what I had for lunch, I'd think, "I usually drink milk," so I'd probably say, "Milk." Now I don't let my memory ruin my life. I just try to keep doing what I'm doing and not think about something else. Losing memories is like when you cut a tree down, you should plant another one. When I can't remember, I

make new memories. I just do something else and put it in my memory instead.

Remembering Things on a Tree Stump

When someone steps on a stump,
It remembers when it was a tree,
With all the kids climbing on it.
The sound of little birds hatching
Makes the tree stump cry.
Birds singing bring memories

Like songs bring memories to me.
It remembers having birds' nests on it,
Eggs hatching in it,
And the mom bringing worms and bugs.
When I stand on it, it remembers when it was cut down,
All the kids that used to climb on it
And cut its bark with their knives,
Like when I had the stroke.
The tree couldn't sway and I couldn't speak.
I stand on it and it reminds me
Of drinking shiny water at nighttime
Because of its roots when it rains soft drops.
It reminds me of popcorn because I'm waiting for Dahlia to bring me
    some.
It cannot remember when it was chopped
Down because it's a bad time.
It's getting more tired and more tired of remembering the sad parts.
Me planting a new tree would make the stump feel leaves growing.
It could hear birds singing and feel like a teenager again.

I'm tired of bad memories too. It's sort of good to forget the bad stuff because you don't have to remember the pain you went through. I know it's there but I have more good memories of being sick, like when for my birthday, I got to go to this gymnastics show at Villanova with Lance Ringnold. Or when I came home from the hospital, or getting cards and George, a stuffed bear. I thought he was a gorilla at first, so I named him George of the Jungle.

IT'S not true that without a memory you have no personality, because memory has nothing to do with personality. Personality is the way you act, it's not what happen*ed*, it's what's happen*ing*, *while* you're doing it. It's if you're sad or hyper, like me. Memory is the past, and the past is the past. I try not to think about that because it wasn't a very good past. A lot of it was, but not the recent past. The present is totally cool because I'm all better and I can do what I want, mostly, and now I can walk without a cane and my hair is growing back so people won't stare at me anymore — or not as much, anyway. When I was bald and people started staring, I wanted to yell some bad words at them. Now people sometimes stare at my leg, or at my brace if I'm wearing shorts.

Not having a normal memory doesn't really bother me except when I'm taking tests. But if I'm taking a spelling test and I can't remember a definition, I'll just think real hard and then make one up. Like, "debauchery" is kind of like archery except you use poles instead of arrows, or "loquacious" means a kind of green, tangy salad dressing.

I think I'm smart, but school just doesn't appreciate someone like me. I'm definitely not smart in the way they want me to be. School thinks a smart kid is a boy who wears a tie and is really into science. They want you to not have cool clothes and to pay attention to your studies and listen to Bach and classical music and to have a good memory. You have to have a good memory to be able to sequence, which is one of the things I can't do. If I get a list of things, I can't put it in order, or remember a story in order. Sequencing is important if you're a businessman, so you can put things, like your meetings and papers and stuff, in order. I can't do that but I read very well and know lots of hard words, twelfth-grade words. It's just that I see the book, and there are things going on and then they disappear into the back of my mind, like smoke. Forgetting books doesn't really matter because the fun is in the reading, not the remembering. My all-time favorite book is *Just As Long As We're Together* about these friends that walk to school and then they start becoming teenagers and they talk on the phone so much.

School thinks that an education is an education and nothing more. I think that education is knowing how to make poems like I do and it's being able to sing without making your voice squeaky. That used to happen to me a lot, but now I know how to do it. When you want to go low, you lift your head high, and when you want to go high, you put your head down.

I know more than most of the kids in the learning-disabled classes because I was in the A-section before and that helps me a little bit. But they don't appreciate that, and since I can't keep up with the A-level anymore, they put me in the C-level, which I think sucks. Those kids are slower to learn, and they make me mad because they don't want to learn. I want to learn but I'm slow because I can't remember, and the C-level doesn't help me with my memory. My mom says I'm working with a memory retrainer, but I'm not sure I've met her yet.

SOMETIMES, if I know I can't remember something, I just refuse to do it, like when they want me to take a test. I get mad because I know I used to be able to do it and now I can't. Even if I study, it's just like, "Oh my God! I've never seen this before!" I can't choose which thing goes first. My teachers can make me do it over and over and over again, but even the third time I won't remember it. When I try to sequence, it's black in my head and there's a bit of light, like the sun shining at camp, with pictures in the back of my head, but no order. I just do what I can. I had to use an encyclopedia to help me with this poem:

Yeah, Right. Sure I Remember This Stuff

George Washington became president in 1789.
There was a Great Fire in London in 1666.
Henry Wadsworth Longfellow wrote *Paul Revere's Ride*.
The Inca Empire built a fortress called Sacsahamun.

"Now Katie, do you remember all this?"
Yeah, right. Sure I remember this stuff.

Georges Seurat painted *Baignade* in 1883.
Gandhi's independence movement was in 1947.
Ivan the Terrible doubled his empire in 1544.
Michael Romanov was elected czar in 1613.

"Do you think you can take this test now, Katie?"
Yeah, right. Sure I remember this stuff.

4000 divided by 321 equals 12.461059.
The capital of Kansas is Topeka.

"Did you study the material I assigned, Katie?"
Yeah, right. Sure I remember this stuff.

BUT dark green jellybeans taste like watermelon.

And Nadia Comaneci got the first 10 in women's gymnastics.
Richard Marx is cute, a great voice, and I love his music.
And Candied Peach lipstick tastes like drinking smooth cream.

Now teachers, you better memorize *those* facts by Monday.

If I didn't have my aide, Lisa, at school to help me, I'd have trouble finding classrooms and knowing what we were doing, but it's hard because with someone always there I can't get to talk to boys. It's funny that I start writing in the middle of the page. It looks like the left side to me because I can't see out of the left side of my eyes because of the stroke. Also, the brain tumor destroyed some part of my vision and now I can't see out of that part. They call that "left field cuts" because your left field of what your eye sees is cut out.

In Left Field

I don't have a left field.
I used to see only half-things.
Half-lamps, half-chairs, half-people.
The other half was piña colada white
And fuzzy.
Standing at home plate, I
Can't see left field behind third base.
Standing in left field, there's
No home plate.
For a while, I was out in left field.
On hospital food I hallucinated ants all
Over me.
Ants on the walls, names for them all.
George, Annie, Brendan.
Without a left field in left field,
They were
orge,
nie, and
ndan.
Left field without a left field is just
A field . . .

Of wildflowers in rainbow order,

without an order,
　　Smells like vanilla perfume.

　　　　　　　　Pillows of grass
　　　　　　　　in greens and purples.

A little
　　smoke-gray field mouse,
　　　　　　　robins hopping around.
A rabbit as white as the moon.

　　　　　　　A breeze like the ocean.

　　　A field of
　　　pinkish-purple
　　　hope, growing like love.

　　　　　　　Each petal is a wish.

My sister Jenn did the drawing for that poem. Her real name is Jennifer the Brat. That's not true. Actually, her *real* middle name is Christina. Jennifer Christina the Brat Martin. She's fourteen. I am Katie Louise the Great Martin. My parents only had one great kid. Jenn always tells on me when I curse. I try not to, but I do curse a lot. I like to drive Jenn crazy mostly because she's my sister, but I definitely have to teach her to live in the real world somehow. She goes to the Hole in the Wall Gang Camp, too, for siblings camp. This poem is one I wrote for Jenn:

> Dear Jenn,
>   I just wanted to tell you
> I'm sorry I teased
> you and called you names
> I'm sorry I said "Duhhhh"
> when you got words mixed up.
>   And when I called you
> boogerface.
>   But it was funny when
> you huffed like a blowfish.
> And stomped in your room like a herd
> of turtles.
> Hiding in your shell.
>   Love, your sister always, Katie!

I live with my mom, my dad, my sister, and two babies that we foster called Bernie and Allie. We also have Spike and Buzz the cats, and a dog called Bear. I think lots of people leave stray pets near our house because they know we'll take care of them. My brother Bernie and my sister Allie are really cute and it's good to foster kids because they have better homes and they don't get battered. We've fostered two other kids before we got Bernie. You just have to try not to get too attached. If you do, then one day you might not want to do it again.

I REALLY love music, I have always loved it. In the hospital, I listened to music all the time. When I felt bad, I used to listen to rowdy music that cleared my mind from bouncing around and made me feel better. I mostly like soft rock, but I like Bon Jovi, too, and he's not soft rock. Certain songs make me cry. I don't know why and it makes me mad because I can't sing them when I'm crying and I love them so much. "Somewhere

over the Rainbow" and "Puff the Magic Dragon" and "Lean on Me" make
me cry. "You've Got a Friend" makes me cry hard because it reminds me
of my grammy and of friends in the hospital. "The Wind Beneath My
Wings" makes me cry because of my sister Jenn, because I always got the
spotlight. In some ways, life is the wind beneath my wings because remembering what has happened has made me want to live life even better.
I wanted to die but now I don't. I know lots of James Taylor songs. I like
Nelson, they're so cute. I like blond hair on boys. I wouldn't want to live
in California because — "POW!" — people get shot there, but I'd love to
visit, buy cool, California-style clothes, and bring back a cute California
boyfriend.

    I think I like boys so much because they're different from us, but
people, too. I'm gonna be a major-league baseball player, the first woman.
But I'll have an unfair advantage — I'll be able to go in the men's locker
room. Or maybe I could be a football coach. I'd get to pat all those guys
on the butt. That would be great! There should be a woman president because women are more sensible. Actually, maybe it should be me.

I LOVE makeup. I have tons of it. I love blush and lipstick best, glossy colors. I like it because you can do anything with it, and then take it off, and it makes you look pretty and more mature. Except it's sort of hard to do it with one hand, especially eyeliner. Makeup is like a mask that gives you a better feeling about yourself.

Makeup
I love to design faces
Outrageous, wet-looking, sparkly, wild
light pink lipstick
purple eggplant parmesan eyeshadow
Expressing myself.

I used to be more daring before I was sick, I think. At school I used to do back handsprings on the ground. Now the most daring thing I can do is somersaults, but that's pretty dangerous because the way I do it, I could hurt my neck really bad. I just flip and then I flop on my left side. So I don't do those much, but I like to skip. The way I skip, it's not really like skipping but it's *my* way of skipping. Before I was sick I liked to play base-ball, like I do now. I liked to roller skate. That's too much now. One thing I really miss that I used to do before I had the stroke was sliding down banisters.

Banisters

Sliding down was so
  much fun
    lips laughing with drunkenness
    wind blowing in my face
    with spirit everywhere
      blond hair locks in my eyes
        Flowing down was wonderful
          Climbing up over and over again.
            Sickening with time; praying
            for life to be saved
            From disease, spreading
            like wildflower fire.

I think most of the time I'm more sad than mad, probably. Not doing gymnastics is the worst. I always wanted to be a gymnast, an Olympic champion. I had posters of Mary Lou Retton — she trained at the same gym as me, Berks Gym — and I had pictures of me on team and ribbons all over my wall. We took them down after the stroke. It was sort of de-pressing to have them, I think. I can look at the pictures of me in gymnastics or on team without crying now, but when I watch gymnastics on TV, I sometimes feel like crying because I'm not able to do it anymore.

Tumbling

Over and over, over and over.
Cartwheels like a windmill,
Handsprings like dolphins,
Aerials like oak leaves, flipping in the fall.
Over and over, over and over again.

Practice and repeat until it's drilled into your mind.
Always look up.
Never stop smiling.

Whatever happens, land on your feet.
Point your toe and be proud of who you are.

On the beam you have to center:
Eyes directly in front of you and choose one thing.
If you look down, you fall down.
I just needed one finger behind me, to know someone was there.
Later, that was my mom in the hospital.
My center then was life.

Over and over, over and over.
Cartwheels like a windmill,
Handsprings like dolphins,
Aerials like oak leaves, flipping in the fall.
Over and over, over and over again.

On the bars, you needed straight arms, but not too straight.
You had to cast off, snap yourself into the bar.
Like snapping into reality.

Practice and repeat until it's drilled into your mind.
Always look up.
Never stop smiling.
Whatever happens, land on your feet.
Point your toe and be proud of who you are.

On the floor, my favorite,
You could go faster and higher.
You have to go down lower to get higher.
You have to get sick to enjoy life after.
You have to learn dance to do floor.
I was just starting to dance when I had to stop team.

Over and over, over and over.
Cartwheels like a windmill,
Handsprings like dolphins,
Aerials like oak leaves, flipping in the fall.
Over and over, over and over again.

When I lived in Alabama, I was in a gymnastics show, I was three or
four, I think, and in the middle of my routine, my shoe flew off. So I didn't
know what to do and I stopped in the middle of my routine and was looking around and everybody was laughing and I just ran out and got my

shoe. That was at Wilcox Academy in Alabama. See, I remember things that are way, way back, like when I was three. It's the things that just happened, I don't remember as well.

NOW I'm gonna tell my story the way I think it happened. It's not exactly like my mom's version because I don't see things the way she does. The order comes out all jambled up, but I'll do my best to remember.

When I was ten or eleven, I think I was eleven, I had bad headaches. I was walking into walls and corners because I couldn't see. I was having trouble at school and they say I was angry at the teachers but I don't remember that part. Oh, I sort of do. I remember telling the teacher that I *can't* do math and I *won't* do it because I can't. I was yelling. I couldn't see to do it and it made me mad so I yelled.

At gymnastics, we were learning to do back walkovers on the beam and I was scared because I couldn't see and I was crying and crying and I freaked out at Miss Shelley. I couldn't explain to them why I couldn't do it because I didn't know. They wanted to help me, but they didn't know how to.

I Will Sing Life

MY mom took me to the eye doctor and right away he diagnosed me with a brain tumor — as soon as he looked in my eye. And he took my mom out of the room and told her and it really scared me. No, he took me out of the room and told my mom. He told me to go play a game, which was really another eye test. Always tricking me. When my mom told me, I started crying. I didn't know, but I thought it was a sack of water in my brain. That's what it is, sort of. Now I know that cancer is if you have a tumor or if you have blood cancer. I knew that cancer could kill you because my grandmother and grandfather had cancer, till they died.

The scariest part was when I thought I was gonna die. That felt like a knife in my heart. I asked, "When am I going to die?" and I wondered what my friends were going to do without me because I thought they'd be sad. My mom comforted me. I don't really remember what she said but she gave me hope. I wouldn't have made it without her. She helped me and she saved me. She stayed by my bed the whole time and she cried with me, she comforted me and I comforted her in the rough times. I feel bad that she cried, but I knew I couldn't help it and I wish it wasn't so hard on her but it helped us to be together. My dad's a really funny guy and a really great guy. He was working real hard when I was sick. He had to pay for my bills. But when he was working in Philadelphia, he'd come visit me after work. That was neat.

AFTER I was diagnosed, I had brain surgery. It was a biopsy and they take a piece of the tumor and see if it's cancer, which mine was. I think I remember going into the operating room and I called the doctor. . . . Oh no. That was my mom when she had a baby. But I called my doctor something funny, I think. All I really remember was getting the sleeping medicine. That was cool. It made me feel dizzy and stuff but it's weird: I like feeling dizzy sometimes. Like, I love standing up and spinning in circles.

When I had my tumor, I got radiation. Radiation is a form of electricity that can either cause cancer or get rid of cancer. I don't know how it does that but the lady who discovered radiation somehow spilled something on her hands and she died. The radiation made my hair fall out. I was in the tub taking a bath one day and I was washing my hair and all of a sudden, I noticed that my hair fell out. I looked at my hand and there was this whole big clump of hair in my hand and it was really scary. I knew it happened sometime or another, but I wasn't expecting it then. I screamed and screamed 'cause it scared me. I just kept pulling it out because I wanted to get it over with. It was just coming out all over the tub.

It was gross. It was to my shoulder then. They had to wash the tub. After that I wore hats. People stared at me, especially since I was in a wheel-chair. I think I was in the chair for a long time after the stroke.

When I was in the hospital, I got tons of cards. And I got some from people I didn't even know. That was good, it was nice to know that people cared. I think when you send a card to someone who just got diagnosed with cancer, you shouldn't overdo it and say: "Don't worry, it'll be okay, it'll be all right," because then it makes them worry that you're just saying it to make them feel better. The best thing to do is just act normal and say, "How's your cancer?" It's real bad when people come in and start to cry. It makes you think you're in really bad shape and that you might not live and it gets you down and you might start crying too and get sicker. It was okay when my mom cried though, we cried together.

The Child Life workers at the hospital were great, especially Danielle. She was really really cool. They took us to the zoo or to museums instead of sitting in the hospital all day. They almost made it fun for us to be in the hospital.

AFTER that I was hallucinating because my electrolytes were screwy. I re-member thinking there were ants all over me and I would keep brushing them off, I think. I hallucinated about cats on the walls and I named all the cats.

KIDS with cancer get a lot of stuff from places like the Make-A-Wish Foun-dation. I got a shopping spree, and a bunch of CDs and makeup and a Caboodle and a lap harp. It seems unfair to the healthy kids that we get so much stuff and free tickets and things, but I think it's good to get what you can, while you can. Those other kids are gonna live forever. Anyway, those places can't make all your wishes come true. I wrote this poem last sum-mer about my wishes. It's one of the first ones I ever wrote:

> And then I was a tall tree
> that could move around and use all its body parts and now it
> would be a normal tree.
> If a branch fell off, part of the tree would be doing flips and
> the branches were doing a routine and the trunk was
> swaying to the music.

I was always funny, I think. My sense of humor got better, though, from all the jokes they told me to cheer me up when I was sick. I made this joke up myself: How did God name woman? When He looked at her He said "Whoa, man!" I made that up.

I got lots of medicine, like steroids that were weird. They made my cheeks puff out and I was hungry all the time. I always wanted to have potato chips and popcorn and salty things. I know I took prednisone, hydrocortisone, and a lot of other ones but I can't really remember. Prednisone made me really wild. It made me feel horrible. The medicine wasn't what made me depressed, not really. Just having cancer made me depressed sometimes.

My family called me "Chunky Monkey" then because I was fat from the steroids. Jenn called me Little Sinéad when I was bald, and I didn't appreciate that. I mean, I like Sinéad O'Connor, but not *that* much. I didn't like the "Little" part either. I see the pictures of me that way, with a fat face and no hair, and I know it's me but I don't remember that stuff. It just doesn't bother me. I try not to think about it. When I grow up, I'm gonna be pretty, but I'm gonna be cool. I wonder if I ate lunch yet.

I DON'T really remember having the stroke. My mom just found me. She told all the doctors that I had a stroke. They didn't believe her. She always likes to read doctor books and stuff. Some kids don't understand why my left hand can't work. I tell them that I had a stroke in my brain and it affected my left side. It will get better but I don't think I'll ever be able to use my left hand like my right hand, or maybe not even at all. That makes me mad sometimes, like I can't play the piano or run anymore. Sometimes, when I look at my left arm, I get sad. I used to hate it and I sort of still do, sometimes. I just wish it would work.

Sides

To me, my left side is imaginary.
It's there but it isn't.
It's there because you can see it, and sometimes I feel things.
The sensations are kooky though, water is colder and hurts hurt
    more.
My personality is like my right side. I like to bounce like a tram-
    poline.
My left side can't do anything. It just hangs.
I try to ignore my left side.

My right side is a tiger. It races around and eats roller skates.
My left side is a sloth, it sleeps all day.
My right side is red inside, warm and hyper.
My left side is blue and cold and stiff inside and tied to a stick.
My right side roars.
My left side chatters like a guinea pig.
My right side's name would be Elvira.
My left side would be Patty.

My right side does the wild thing dance.
My left side is a minuet.
My right side breathes like a hot air balloon with a lot of air.
My left side breathes like a person on a respirator, weak and
    can't talk.
My right side dreams about boys.
My left side dreams about scary nightmares of people getting
    killed and cut-up bodies,
My right side will teach my left side to smile right,
My left side will teach my right side to be gentle.
My right side is right about everything.
My left side has been left behind.

I only smile with my right side. My left side doesn't go up, but I can push it up with my hand. I wish I could smile right. I think that when I'm smiling, my left side is sleeping and dreaming of trying to smile.

AFTER the stroke I was on a ventilator. I wanted to die then. I cried a lot when I had cancer because I was afraid to die and I didn't want to, but then when I had the stroke, it was so horrible that I wanted to die. I couldn't be active and couldn't talk, couldn't even write. I don't really remember what I thought, but I think that inside I thought normally. I couldn't communicate in any way or react to anything. It was really silent. Like I was dead. One day when the ventilator was on I was mad and I said, "I can't breathe with this damn thing!" Oh, maybe I could talk then, because I said that, and anyway, I ripped it out. Then I did have a near-death experience. I pulled out the ventilator because I saw my grandmother calling me from Heaven because I was dying. I could see her face and she was really fuzzy and blurry and I said, "Take me with you, Grammy! Take me with you!" because I was dying and wanted to die. It bothers me that I can't remember all of it.

When I first stood up when I was off the ventilator, I started to cry because I was so happy. Because it was possible I would never walk again. Then I went to rehab for a long time and learned to walk and talk again. I went to physical therapy and occupational therapy and speech therapy and said, "I can do this," even when I couldn't because it hurt too much.

I think I appreciate life more now because I saw Heaven and I thought I was going to die. I know life is a whole lot better than death because I've seen friends die. After that I thought, "I can't cry all my life so I'd better get to work on living."

Katie
Martin

Seize life for pizza and meeting new friends.
Pinch life for seeing babies and eating Crackerjacks.
For the light and the heat and the life of sunshine.
Eat life to drink coffee and for horses.
Jump at life to see flowers and the American flag,
To smell the dew that is like blue gobstoppers.
Dream up life for the zoo, and bunny rabbits and tickly feathers.
For coffee ice cream and guinea pigs.
Live for the hippopotamus.
I live for blueberry bubblegum and makeup,
For elephants without the smell and playing pool.
Write poems in life for chocolate mint jelly beans
and the smell of spaghetti.
Jump over life for gymnastics, swimming in a blue pool
and loose, bright clothes.
For Whitney Houston singing "The Greatest Love of All"
because kids need to know they're important.
Give life flowers for cute, handsome, tall boys kissing me.
For a round-off, back handspring, back tuck
and bright, tight, hot pink leotards.
For singing "Lean on Me."
Devour life for the romantic adventures that make life delicious.

Camp is a place where you learn to live life better because you can do all sorts of things you thought you'd never do again, like fishing, or horseback riding, because it's hard getting on a horse even without a stroke. Camp teaches you that you can do other things than lie in a hospital bed or lie in a grave forever. I think it's real cool that it doesn't cost anything because the kids don't have much money left because they paid all the hospital bills. And it's great that they can finally go have fun. And live while they can. I met new people and it's so good to meet other sick kids because they can help you through when you're having trouble and you help them when they're down. Like I helped David. He was really crying 'cause he had cancer in his brain and I talked to him and I cheered him up. He was so cute, I just couldn't resist. I told him my story, that I had a brain tumor and I got radiation and now it's all gone. It made him feel better because I gave him hope that he'll be better. The best part of

I Will Sing Life

cheering somebody up is that you've got a good friend. And maybe when you're down, he'll cheer you up. I don't care if my boyfriend has no hair because I was like that, too. I'm not afraid to see it.

Camp is cool because Paul Newman comes and visits. I met him at dinner and he talked to me and then came back to our cabin. He's cool but Jimmy and Billy are the cutest guys at camp. I think that hope and love and laughing and confidence are all over camp; in a way they're growing as much as the grass is.

Feeling Flowers

Hope has green leaves that you can chew and taste minty.
Hope has little purple flowers that grow on a vine.
If hope is near someone's house, it grows fast
Because there are lots of people around
To give it hope and for it to give hope.
In a field or a forest, packs of deer make it grow faster.
There's always hope growing somewhere.

Love is as red as a snowman's nose.
Love is lots of little plants that grow into a love tree.
They all love each other so they grow more.
They grow near a church or near someone's home.
Or special places where people go to kiss.

Hate is a big black flower the size of a peach.
Hate doesn't grow. It wasn't meant to be, so it just sits there.
You have to burn hate, by bringing your boyfriend there.
It grows in the dark, black city slums.
Inside, it's really white, but it's turned black from all the soot
    and hate.

Laughing is bright red and yellow and its stems are bright
    green.
The leaves are bright blue.
Laughing grows near a candy store.
It's as tall as a puppy and the flowers are round. They smell like
    chocolate cherries.
It grows when kids play guess-your-mother's-age and hide-and-
    seek.

Pain is sort of bushy but not really.
Pain is forest green and hurts to touch from the spines all over it.
Pain grows near funny-smelling white hospitals.
When it hears someone cry or die
It gets bigger and its leaves burst out from inside the stem.

Confidence is a bush with big white flowers, as big as the palms
　　of your hand.
It grows near swimming pools and gymnasiums and running
　　tracks.
It smells sweet like cotton candy.
The flowers are soft as a duck.
It feels people running and tumbling and that makes it grow.

One thing I know is that I can make life even better. When I'm sad,
like when I heard that Corey Svien died, I'll say: "Well, at least he's having
a better life in Heaven." I don't take life for granted anymore. Corey helps
me believe in Heaven and helped me get through hard times. I wish I had
gotten to know him better. When it was his time, he went. God doesn't let
people suffer so He took Corey into His arms. I can't see how anybody can
not believe in Heaven. I've believed in it for all my life. In Heaven, nothing hurts, there's no war, everybody loves everybody. God is your father,
especially when you're up in Heaven, living in His house. If you do get
hurt, God saves you. His house is open to everybody. If you need to talk to
Him you can just call Him, or fly over. I like flying better. You don't really
need wings, you just float over to Him. You can do whatever you want
there, but you can't curse in Heaven. That won't be a problem for me
because I only curse when I get mad or hurt myself and that won't happen
in Heaven.

I THINK that when Corey and Wiz Bear got to Heaven, they saw lots of
flashing lights and then a big flash of purple. They saw God. His hair was
white and His beard was white and He was wearing all purple. Corey felt
no pain anymore. He said, "I can run, I'm okay, I'm alive!" God welcomed
him and gave him new clothes instead of hospital pajamas. He gave him a
silky white robe, like the priests wear.

Then God took them to their own house. It was huge. Of course, it
was green. The carpets were really deep green. Everything was really deep
green and natural colors. The first thing Corey did was start jumping on

I Will Sing Life

his bed. Then he was dreaming and he woke up and he was in a purple room because the sun went down.

I like to think that Wiz Bear in Heaven would make other bears for people not in Heaven. He'll wish for other bears and they'll pop up. My bear would be a gymnast. It would be Jimminy Bear, and its symbol would be a person on a balance beam doing a trick. Wiz would send it down to me on a beam of light and plop! it's on my waterbed. I would keep it forever and have Corey with me forever.

I wrote this poem while I was at camp and so was Corey. It's sort of about him in a way. I didn't know when I wrote it that it was about him, but somehow I did. Poems don't come from what you think you're thinking about.

Clouds

I see the clouds in the water.
They look like cotton balls.
They look more wrinkly than the ones in the sky.
On the other side of the clouds, baby clouds are playing.
On the other side of the other clouds, baby fish are playing.
    The clouds are playing tag.
    The fish are playing shark.
That wrinkly cloud looks like someone with big lips and spiky hair.
Clouds and islands are both new places.
Sort of paradise places.
Reflections from under water look a little bit different,
But almost the same.
When people die, they go to the clouds.
The ones that move are the ones that are occupied.
God tells them where to go.
He looks down at the earth and sees who is sad and who needs
To be cheered up by a beautiful day.
Everyone has a cloud.
That's mine up there,
Hi Grammy, Hi Aunt Edna.
Last night it took a long time for them to cheer me up.
It took Grammy a while to get on her feet.

It was raining the day she died.
The me inside is never gonna die.
I'll go to Heaven and ride white horses.
Everything in Heaven is white.
Except the black people there.

Katie
Martin

Anthology of Poems by Campers from the Hole in the Wall Gang Camp

~~~~~~~~~~~~~~~~~~~~~~~~~~

THE PREVIOUS CHAPTERS have provided an opportunity to hear only seven of the hundreds of voices that make up the Hole in the Wall Gang Camp; the following anthology is an introduction to the work of many more. In the poetry writing program at camp, we start by playing games to get the campers excited about poetry. Then we usually suggest that each camper find a solitary spot in the woods in which to write. When everyone is finished, we gather in a circle and hear what has been written. . . .

How Does a Leaf Feel

How does a leaf feel to be touched by the sun?
Like a child being tickled for the very first time.
How does a leaf feel to be danced upon by ants?
Like a host in his glory, knowing that his guests are content.
How does a leaf feel when it's stroked by a human?
Scared, like a shy child being introduced to a stranger.
And how does a leaf feel when the frost starts to come?
Like a child being struck by a terrible disease and trying his best to
      be brave and survive.

KORREEN BOYD

I Wish

I wish there was a bird from God
     and got me well
from His wings on me,
     and got me well.

JASON ORCUTT

Bug Spray

Bug spray is like the walls we build around ourselves
to protect against fear and pain.
And like these fragile walls, it never really works.

KATE BERGERON

195

I will Sing Life

It Was Alive and Well

It was alive and well
Then one day
When a cold wind blew
It fell, it's dead
It doesn't have a choice.
It would land far away from the tree,
Because the wind would blow it there.
It would journey down to the ground,
Dry up and disappear.
A child has a jacket
A child getting dizzy trying to catch.
But the leaves' angles swerve all over.
He doesn't catch any but makes them into a pile
And plays with them afterwards.
I wish I was a little kid again
To play with the leaves
Because instead of being dead and lifeless
They would seem alive.

DOUG ALLEGRINI

Dear Bush

Dear Bush:
I am sorry that I pulled your leaf off
But I was tempted to write this poem.
But look what happened,
You are now president.

UNSIGNED

Mr. Tree

Mr. tree, why are you leaning?
Because we want to tell our secrets more quietly.

FREDDY HALL

L'espoir

Les nuages, c'est comme la neige,
le soleil comme une orange,
c'est une histoire de l'espoir.
La pluie comme des larmes,
les oiseaux sont amoureux
comme la mer imagine de l'espoir,
ne pas être triste comme des choses.
VALERIE COSSEC

Nature Is Wild

Nature is wild and very quiet.
The wind passes by it
As you look in the middle.

Nature has ferocious beasts
That you hear softly through the breeze,
In the hot, hot summer.
ELIZABETH BALL

The Field

I am, some say, the beauty of the earth.
Some say I am just another place to build another building.
Rather, I think of myself as a woman.
I have the grace, the beauty
My flowers around me, rose, daisy, lilac,
The bees buzzing and birds chirping.
Singing the harmony songs around me.
For I am a field.
MATTHEW NICOLI

I will
Sing Life

I Walked in the Woods

I walked in the woods one day,
when a little ant started to say,
"Get off me, you thoughtless human,
your foot is
on my butt."
PAUL WILLIAMS

A Rainbow

Is a trail of light to the
Other side of the world holding
In straight lines the colors of beauty,
Darkness, glory and hope.
JONNIE WARREN

Katie's Love

Katie's love is flowing like a river
through the hearts in the blue cabin, especially mine.
She's as beautiful as a spring day.
If everybody was a leaf
the amount of Katie's lovers and friends would fill 500 trees
499 of those trees would be filled with my leaves for my likeness of
        you.
Her hair looks like a golden waterfall from all angles.
For me, Katie is fun to have around, like a teddy bear to children.
Every time I think of the Hole in the Wall Gang Camp, I'll think of
        you.
SEAN WILSON

Dear Rock

Dear Rock,
I'm sorry that I moved you and hurt you but I tripped on you.
Call me at 235-4056 home when I leave.
ARMANDO SANDOVAL

The Summer Lake

The
floating
wind
blowing
fish
in
swimming
water
lily pads
in
waves
are
bluish
and
calm.
AREEN ARMENIAN

Laughing

Laughing
are
trees
for
the
poems
I
am
writing.
ROB MONAHAN

I Will Sing Life

Through the Wall

Through the wall
upon the greens
            first
shades of brown
a step closer
            red
            orange
a feather
            attached to
the wing
belonging
to the wind.

TAMARA LYNCH

Hair hair everywhere
in my lap and on my chair.

RENA PARAB

The Rain

The rain is like a snake sliding.
The rain is like dogs thumping their tails on the floor.
When rain drops on my hand it feels like autumn leaves falling.
Rain looks magnetic when it falls to the ground.
When rain falls, it sounds like a ripple.
When I stand in the rain and some drops on my finger, it feels like
Someone dropped a penny on my finger.
When rain slides off a leaf, it reminds me of going down a slide.

RENA PARAB

I Will Fly to Him

I wish there was no beer in the world
I wish I was a bird
I will fly to him and God will come and take it all

MONTRELL TOMPKINS

Islands

A lake of tranquility,
A torrent stream,
My salvation,
And a mother's heart.

I cool with the thought of a strange smile,
Relax with the warm glowing sun,
Shiver from a cool autumn breeze.
But she is my solid ground.
She brings me back home.
She brings me peace.

A rock of great sturdiness,
A river of fantastic beauty,
A small escape in the center,
And I call that home.

JEANNIE MCBREARTY

A Dolphin

A dolphin swimming in an endless sea,
struggling through each new obstacle.
A clump of seaweed,
garbage thrown by a careless fisherman.
A shark's ravenous jaws.
Streams of fishing nets.
A tornado, stronger than the most powerful steam shovel.
Scared, worried, unsure of what's to come.
Tough though,
fighting, fighting.
Until one day she just couldn't anymore.
She wished to be in a place where she didn't have to fight for every
    inch.
And her wish was granted.

JENNIFER MASI

I Will Sing Life

Danielle

Danielle, my little friend
but she had an old soul.
Her voice, that of a child,
young, innocent, yet all knowing.
How many times did she shout through
the wall of the Bone Marrow Transplant unit:
"Hey, Jenny, ya throwin' up yet?"
Every morning I'd laugh at her working out with Jane Fonda
I'd laugh at the endless hours she'd spend watching *Dumbo*
Carefree, for a moment.

The worry rock sits in my room,
At first I refused it vigorously
Now it is my most treasured possession
Thank you, Danielle, you are a treasure.
I guess you were here to lead,
you did your job here touching so many,
Continuing to touch people through everyone who knew you.
JENNIFER MASI

Cancer Is Not Synonymous with Death

Cancer is not synonymous with death.
"Why don't I get all teary eyed and full of sympathy when I hear
someone has cancer?" you may ask.
Because I know cancer can be treated, cured.
Cancer does not mean death.
Don't be ignorant
Don't be scared.
Don't be worried
Listen, Learn, Understand,
Cancer is not synonymous with death.
Believe me, I know.
JENNIFER MASI

So you have starved me of external life,
you wounded my flesh
and toughened my thoughts
you've deprived birds of food that I offer,
you have weakened my resistance and the will to live.
I am suffering from pain
and my sap is dripping.
I cannot see.
I cannot hear.
No more.

ALASTAIR COCHRANE

So Much Depends

So much depends on the littlest brook
in the biggest forest,
giving life to the tiniest tree,
underneath all creation.
So is the same for the smallest smile,
from one special person,
to one in need of . . . love.

AMY FISKE

Acknowledgments

~~~~~~~~~~~~~~~~~~~~~~~~~~~~~~~

FOR A LONG TIME we only dreamt of this book. We thank the following people for helping this dream come true:

Ray Lamontagne for being our friend, adviser, and hero throughout this year. The contribution of his wisdom, enthusiasm, and generosity to this book is second only to the children's. All the Lamontagnes, including Bert, for always making us feel a part of their wonderful family.

Paul Newman and Joanne Woodward, who realized their dream of a place where children can go to "raise a little hell."

The campers, counselors, staff, and offices of the Hole in the Wall Gang Camp — a standing O.

The Dyson Foundation, the A. L. Mailman Family Foundation, the Newman's Own Foundation, and Paul and Nancy Oppenheimer, who not only generously funded this project, but took a personal interest in it.

Donna Piumetti at Travel Bound for tickets; USAir; Holiday Inn, Jacksonville, Florida; Holiday Inn, Morgantown, Pennsylvania; Sheraton Milford, Massachusetts; and Anne Marie at Pied Piper Travel in Hamlin.

Our insightful and sensitive editors, Roger Donald and Catherine Crawford, whose vision nurtured both forest and trees. Michael Mattil's copyediting and Barbara Werden's design both exhibited an uncommon concern for the children's voices.

Our medical adviser and supporter from the beginning, Dr. Howard Pearson.

Our teachers: Geoffrey Hartman, John Hollander, Donald Faulkner, Harold Bloom, Kevis Goodman, Ian Duncan, and the writings of Anatole Broyard and Oliver Sacks. Kenneth Koch's exceptional books about teaching children to write poetry were the inspiration for our poetry program.

The inspiring doctors, social workers, and counselors: Dr. Warren Andiman, Dr. Lindsay Frasier, Dr. Vita Goie, Drs. James and Elizabeth Man-

I Will Sing Life

del, Dr. Paul Martin, and Dr. Paul Pitel. Judith Costello-DuBois, the social workers from the Albert Einstein clinic, Heidi Haiken, Paula Hinson, Paddy Rosbach and the 52 Association, Joyce Simpson, the support group at the Jimmy Fund, and Mary Tasker.

The many people who gave us legal assistance: Pete Putzel, Daniel Ritter, Julie Hilden, Elizabeth McNamara, Kate Rowe, Jane Rubin, and Mark Davis.

Wendy Batteau, Ann Branson, Rita Rosencrantz, and Paulette Kauffman for publishing advice.

David Coleman, who read our final manuscript with such care. His tireless editing of our chapter introductions enriched the book and taught us much about writing.

Michael Sullivan for transcribing many of the interviews, Nettie Archer, Linda Brown, Graciella Dunn, Colleen Esposito, Lori Ann Napolitano, Chris Taylor, and Dwight Hall at Yale for their gracious assistance, and Jodie Pomino for contributing her word-processing expertise.

For floors to sleep on, strength to draw on, and many insights and suggestions: Becca Allen, Melissa Bell, Wendy and Zoë Benson, Carolyn Bickerton, Chris Brown, Liam Callanan, Jimmy Canton, Heather Cromie, Jonathan Davis, Sevgi Demir for design, the DeWinter family, Jeff Dolven for the idea of a Poetry Trial, Harriet Fennell, David Franklin, Lynn Harris, Jackie Harari, Alex Hay, Tim Hotchner, Hillary Keller, Mr. Kelly, Steve Lakatos, Patty Larkin, Colin Lingle, Alex Lithwick, Barry Lithwick, Hillel Lithwick, Natalie Lithwick, Jeff Maher, Shivaun Manley, Meg Marshall, Bob Miller, Miss O'Sullivan, Brian Paul, Devorah Silverman, Fred Singer, Harry Susman, Gillian Thomas, Gary Turchin, Wendy Whitehill, John and Linda Whitton, Bob Wilkins, Scott Winn, Waichi Wong, Yale classes of 1990 and 1991, C.S.P. '90, and a special thank you to Dr. Marilyn Segal, Nick and Wendy Masi, Rick and Monica Segal, and their families.

Our parents — Toby and Florence Berger, and Harvey and Yvonne Lithwick — our grandparents — Jacob and Rachel Baher, Doris Berger, Belle Cohen, and Rose Lithwick — who nurtured this book with all the love that made us never want to leave childhood in the first place.

Finally, and most important, the families of the campers who welcomed us, cared for us, and shared with us their stories and their strength.

L.B. and D.L.
Paupacken Lake, Pennsylvania

THE HOLE IN THE WALL GANG CAMP was designed and built through the vision and efforts of Paul Newman and a group of dedicated volunteers. It first opened in 1988 to provide an exciting and rewarding camping experience for children who have cancer, leukemia, and other serious blood diseases, who because of their disease, its treatment, or its complications, cannot attend ordinary summer camp. Located on three hundred acres of forest land in northeastern Connecticut, the camp was designed to resemble an Old West logging town of the 1890s, but is also equipped to meet the medical and physical needs of these special children. The buildings, facilities, and site make possible a wide range of activities, including swimming in a heated outdoor pool, boating, canoeing, fishing, horseback riding, nature walks, woodworking, music and theater, arts and crafts, a variety of sports, and overnight camping.

The camp serves children, ages seven to seventeen, from throughout the United States and abroad, but with focus on the northeastern states. The summer program offers four ten-day sessions, with two additional seven-day sessions dedicated to children with specific medical problems. There is no cost to campers.